14004

SURE Trainer™   SURE Employee

D1258346

- Use a No. 2 pencil only.
- Do not use ink, ball point, or felt tip pens.
- Make solid marks that fill the oval completely.

● CORRECT   INCORRECT ⊘ ⊗ ⊖ ⊙

SURE Manager   SURE Trainer™   SURE Employee

SEX

○ Female

○ Male

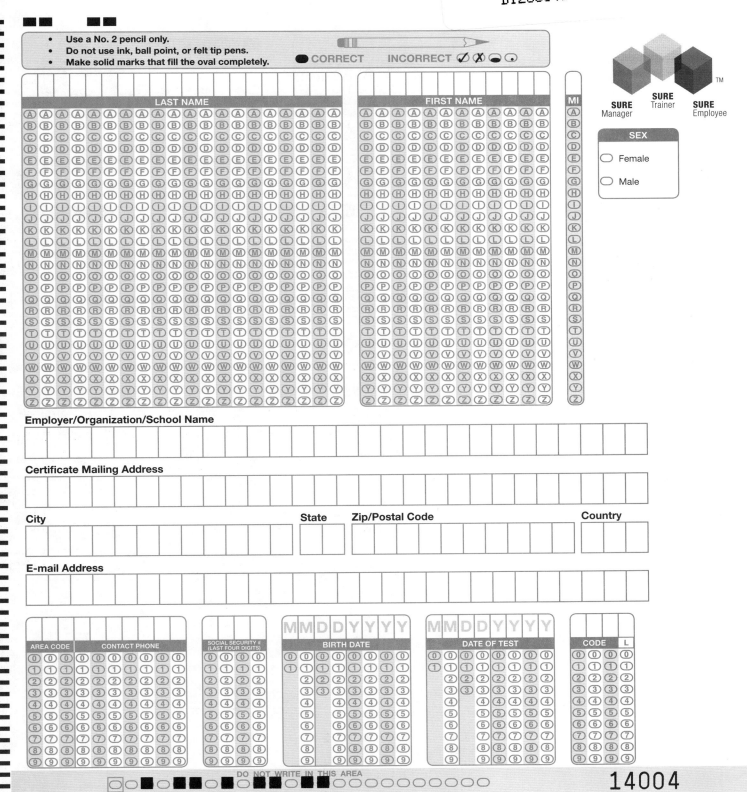

LAST NAME   **FIRST NAME**   **MI**

Employer/Organization/School Name

Certificate Mailing Address

City   **State**   **Zip/Postal Code**   **Country**

E-mail Address

AREA CODE   CONTACT PHONE   SOCIAL SECURITY # (LAST FOUR DIGITS)   BIRTH DATE   DATE OF TEST   CODE   L

M M D D Y Y Y Y   M M D D Y Y Y Y

DO NOT WRITE IN THIS AREA

14004

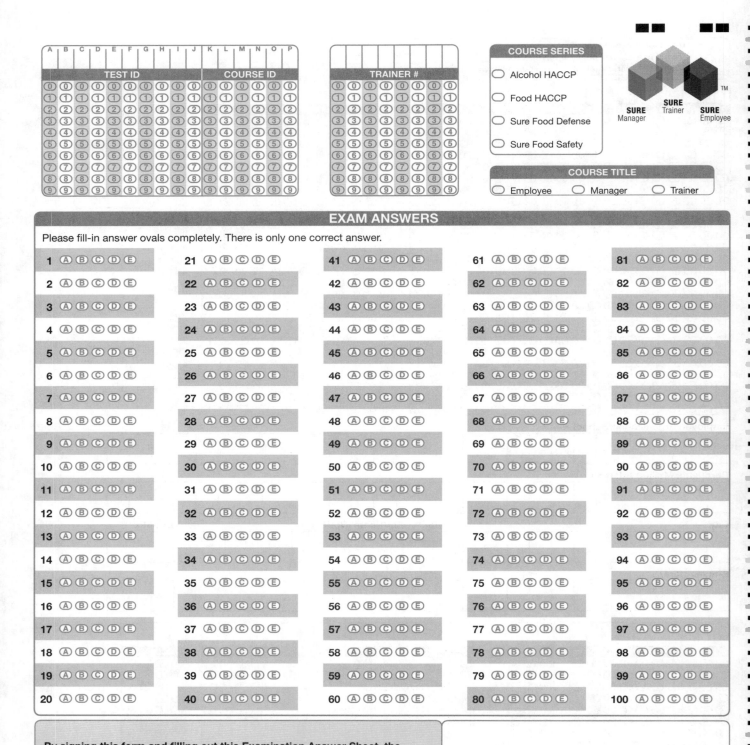

The **HACCP** Food Safety Employee Manual

For food service and retail establishments

Includes 2017 FDA Food Code

Tara DeLotto Cammarata, CP-FS, FMP
Melissa Vaccaro, CP-FS, FMP

Instruis Publishing Company
Perfection through education.

Table of Contents

Introduction

Our Mission

Our Mission is to provide the best possible training material and support to all those who serve and sell products in the food industry. By fulfilling the mission of a HACCP program, the food industry will minimize the risk of contamination of the food served or sold, minimize the risk of foodborne illnesses, and reduce the risk of allergic reactions to food. In studying HACCP, you now are a part of the mission and have an important responsibility in continuing the mission at your food service or retail establishment.

SURE HACCP Food Safety Series

In an effort to better serve the industry and the public, Instruis Publishing Company is proud to introduce The HACCP Food Safety Series. HACCP Food Safety forms another link in the Publishing Company's **SURE** line, which provides the food industry with the finest training material and support. Instruis' **SURE** line provides trainers, managers, and employees **S**afe, **U**seful, **R**esponsible **E**ducation. You can be **SURE** that by using Instruis' comprehensive manuals and support material you are receiving the finest and most interactive material available. The **SURE** HACCP Food Safety Series manuals and support aids have been written and prepared by trainers and food industry leaders who understand the most effective way to train your employees to provide the safest food to your customers.

Instruis Publishing Company's HACCP Food Safety series applies the HACCP principles to food service and retail establishments that serve and/or sell food to improve the industry by providing the material to train **SURE** Employees, **SURE** Managers, and **SURE** Trainers. There are three training manuals in the comprehensive **SURE** Food Safety HACCP program:

- The **HACCP** Food Safety Employee Manual
- The **HACCP** Food Safety Manager Manual
- The **HACCP** Food Safety Trainer Manual

At the conclusion of each course, the **SURE** HACCP Food Safety Program provides a demonstration of knowledge examination which is graded by the publisher to confirm the integrity of the process. Each successful participant receives a certificate and wallet card demonstrating his or her proficiency valid for four years. Employing **SURE** trained individuals allows managers to know that their employees have the core knowledge needed to properly handle food in order to prevent, eliminate, and reduce foodborne illness. Regulators can be confident that the **SURE** trained staff is committed to food safety and HACCP; as well as, up to date on the latest regulatory requirements.

The best way for an employer to be **SURE** that the establishment is fully prepared to meet or exceed the latest regulatory requirements and have the best trained and safest staff is to have every person trained either as a **SURE** Employee, a **SURE** Manager, or a **SURE** Trainer.

How to Use This Book

The **HACCP** Food Safety Employee Manual is the basic book for food handlers and management. This manual serves as the foundation for understanding what HACCP is and its importance to a safe food service or retail establishment. In this manual, you will learn that a complete HACCP system includes prerequisite programs, standard operating procedures, and the 7 HACCP principles. You will learn that using these 7 HACCP principles, along with prerequisite programs and standard operating procedures will prevent, eliminate, and reduce hazards to serve and/or sell safe food.

This book is divided into five sections each represents one of the five points of the star. Each Star Point has the following elements:

- Myth or Fact exercise
- Star Point Goals
- Food for Thought exercise
- Star Point explanation
- Examples
- Star Knowledge exercise
- Pop Quiz
- Check for Understanding exercise
- Conclusion

You are a very important part of the food service or retail industry. We have developed the **"HACCP STAR"** as a training aid to assist in making you the best, most qualified trained person you can be.

HACCP: Star Points to Food Safety

On a clear night, one looks up in the sky and sees the millions of sparkling stars. These millions of sparkling stars are all unique and different, but all play an important role in the universe. Just like one of those millions of stars, you are one of the millions of food professionals and food service or retail operations of the world. But do not be fooled; you are an important part of the preparation and service of safe food in the world. Every operation serving or selling food needs to have a food safety system to protect the food supply. And every establishment needs to put in place a system that is designed specifically for that establishment to guarantee the food being served is safe to eat. You are just as important as any other part in the establishment where you work. How well you do your job makes the difference in serving safe food or risking a foodborne illness. This specific food safety system is called **HACCP** (pronounced "has-sip"); **H**azard **A**nalysis and **C**ritical **C**ontrol **P**oint. HACCP is a system comprised of 7 principles that are to be applied to a written food safety program focusing on the food in your operation. The 7 HACCP principles are:

- **Principle 1:** Conduct a hazard analysis
- **Principle 2:** Determine critical control points
- **Principle 3:** Establish critical limits
- **Principle 4:** Establish monitoring procedures
- **Principle 5:** Establish corrective actions
- **Principle 6:** Establish verification procedures
- **Principle 7:** Establish record keeping and documentation procedures

HACCP is a **proactive approach** to control every step in the flow of food to prevent foodborne illness or injury. What you do or do not do makes a big difference in serving safe food. The goal of HACCP is to **prevent, eliminate, and reduce** food safety problems. Our goal is for you to be a HACCP All-Star!

Following a HACCP plan is very important because it saves lives! The Centers for Disease Control and Prevention (CDC) estimates that every year, 48 million people get sick and 3,000 people die from eating unsafe food. That is 1 in 6 Americans becoming sick annually. The HACCP program requires every team member in the food service or retail industry to be responsible and to ensure that the food he or she prepares, serves, and sells to customers is not hazardous to the consumers health.

Even though typically, as an employee, you are not developing or writing a HACCP plan, you still need to understand the basic knowledge of HACCP in order to effectively carry out your daily duties within the food facility. Understanding HACCP will allow you to understand why you are expected to perform certain tasks and document specific information at your job.

Prerequisite programs such as food safety and food defense **standard operating procedures** (SOPs), are the building blocks for creating an effective HACCP plan. If any team members of the food service or retail operation do not follow these procedures, even the most well thought out HACCP plan will fail. To ensure the development of an effective HACCP plan for your establishment, the basic food safety and food defense standard operating procedures must be reviewed. This will be covered in the first two Star Points or chapters of this book. The book will then cover how a HACCP plan is created and how to use an effective HACCP plan for your food service or retail establishment using the 7 HACCP Principles.

The HACCP Star

The goal of this HACCP training program is to make you, the food service or retail employee, a HACCP All-Star! To be a HACCP All-Star, you must complete all five points of the HACCP Star. Here is the HACCP Star and the five major points that define a successful HACCP system.

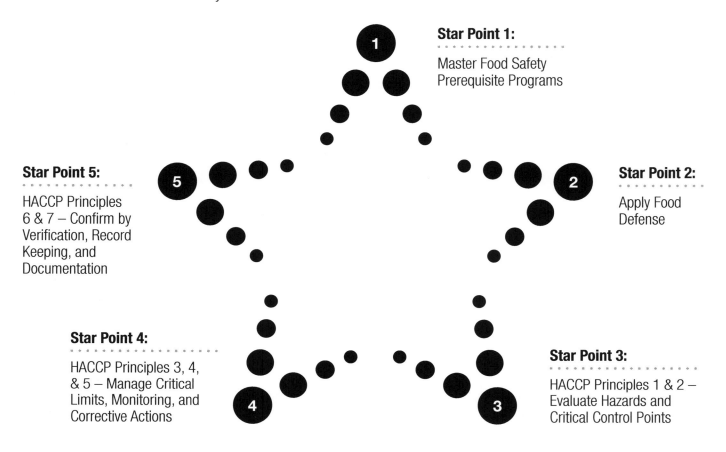

Star Point 1:

Master Food Safety Prerequisite Programs

Star Point 2:

Apply Food Defense

Star Point 3:

HACCP Principles 1 & 2 – Evaluate Hazards and Critical Control Points

Star Point 4:

HACCP Principles 3, 4, & 5 – Manage Critical Limits, Monitoring, and Corrective Actions

Star Point 5:

HACCP Principles 6 & 7 – Confirm by Verification, Record Keeping, and Documentation

HACCP Star
1. Master Food Safety Prerequisite Programs
2. Apply Food Defense
3. HACCP Principles 1 & 2 – Evaluate Hazards and Critical Control Points
4. HACCP Principles 3, 4, & 5 – Manage Critical Limits, Monitoring, and Corrective Actions
5. HACCP Principles 6 & 7 – Confirm by Verification, Record Keeping, and Documentation

Upon successful completion of the **SURE** Employee examination, a certificate and wallet card will be issued. Your **SURE** Employee certificate expires in four years. It is critical to keep your certification current. Once you have read through this entire manual you will be able to:

- Identify the causes of foodborne illnesses;
- Identify the key points of HACCP;
- Explain the 7 HACCP principles;
- Follow prerequisite programs for food safety;
- Apply standard operating procedures for food safety and food defense in your operation;
- Identify the three classifications of recipes;
- Determine Critical Control Points (CCPs);
- Apply correct critical limits;
- Complete monitoring forms;
- Determine effective corrective actions; and
- Understand HACCP verification and record keeping.

This book utilizes the 2017 **United States Food and Drug Administration** (FDA) **Model Food Code**, (Food Code). The Food Code establishes practical, science-based guidance for preventing risk factors that cause foodborne illness. The Food Code is published every four years by the FDA, in conjunction with the CDC, and the U.S. Department of Agriculture (USDA). Every two years, a supplement of information and changes that will be added to the next Food Code is published. This is a model code for state, city, county, and tribal agencies to uniformly regulate restaurants, retail food stores, vending operations, and various food service or retail operations.

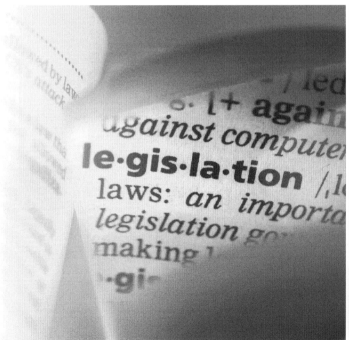 

HACCP Pre-Test (Circle one.)

Now, you will take a HACCP Pre-Test to measure your current food safety, food defense, and HACCP knowledge. It is important to complete this HACCP Pre-Test because this allows the trainer to measure your success as you work toward becoming a HACCP All-Star. Let's get started.

1. **What does HACCP stand for?**
   a. Hazard Associated with Cooking Chicken Products
   b. Hazard Analysis and Critical Control Point
   c. Hazard Analysis Control Critical Points

2. **Conducting a hazard analysis includes answering** _____.
   a. "What is the likelihood of a hazard to occur?" and "What are the standard operating procedures?"
   b. "What is the likelihood of a hazard to occur?" and "What is the risk if the hazard does occur?"
   c. "What is the likelihood of following proper procedures?" and "What is the risk of using hazardous chemicals?"

3. **A critical control point (CCP) is** _____.
   a. an essential step in the product-handling process where controls can be applied and a food safety hazard can be prevented, eliminated, or reduced to acceptable levels.
   b. one of the last chances you have to be sure the food will be safe when you serve or sell it.
   c. both a and b

4. **Record keeping includes** _____.
   a. recording hot holding temperatures in a log book.
   b. records of employee training in food safety and food defense.
   c. both a and b

5. **What is an SOP?**
   a. Single Opportunity Plan
   b. Special Operating Procedure
   c. Standard Operating Procedure

6. **An example of a critical limit is** _____.
   a. cleaning food contact surfaces.
   b. cooking foods to a specific temperature for a specific amount of time.
   c. measuring the limits of how long you can cook food before it burns.

7. **Foods need to be cooked to a specific temperature because** _____.
   a. most people like food well-done.
   b. the right time and temperature is the only way to make sure it's safe to eat.
   c. you do not want to "overcook" the food if you have to warm it up later.

8. **What is RTE?**
   a. Ready-To-Eat
   b. Right through Eating
   c. Ready to Execute

9. **Monitoring procedures are conducted to ensure that** _____.

    a. we are correctly meeting critical limits for the CCPs.

    b. customers are buying the food at the food bar.

    c. discarded food is properly recorded on the profit/loss statement.

10. **Food defense is** _____.

    a. preventing the deliberate contamination of food.

    b. having vendors wear head coverings when delivering food.

    c. a new national government program that reports incidents to the Department of Homeland Security.

11. **An example of a corrective action is** _____.

    a. receiving a written warning.

    b. showing a coworker how to take shortcuts while preparing food.

    c. rejecting a product that does not meet purchasing or receiving specifications.

12. **An employee checking** _____ **is an example of a monitoring activity.**

    a. food temperatures

    b. critical control point records

    c. to make sure the backdoor is closed

13. **What is the temperature danger zone?**

    a. 45°F–140°F (7.2°C–60°C)

    b. 35°F–140°F (1.7°C–60°C)

    c. 41°F–135°F (5°C–57.2°C)

14. **What are the characteristics of time/temperature control for safety of food (TCS)?**

    a. Dry, low acidity, vegetable based

    b. Moist, neutral acidity, protein

    c. Moist, sugary, low fat

15. **Food security is** _____.

    a. a two-year supply of food for a country.

    b. designating an employee to watch the buffet.

    c. a newly appointed government program.

HACCP Pre-Test Results

How many points did you earn? _____

If you scored 14 – 15 points — Congratulations! You are very knowledgeable already about HACCP!

If you scored 9 – 13 points — Good job! You have a basic understanding of HACCP and all of its components.

If you scored 5 – 8 points — There is no time like the present to learn about HACCP! This book will give you a great opportunity to fine-tune your HACCP skills.

If you scored 0 – 4 points — Everyone needs to start somewhere!

It is important to track your progress as you complete each point of the star to earn your HACCP All-Star Certificate!

HACCP Star Point 1:
Master Food Safety Prerequisite Programs

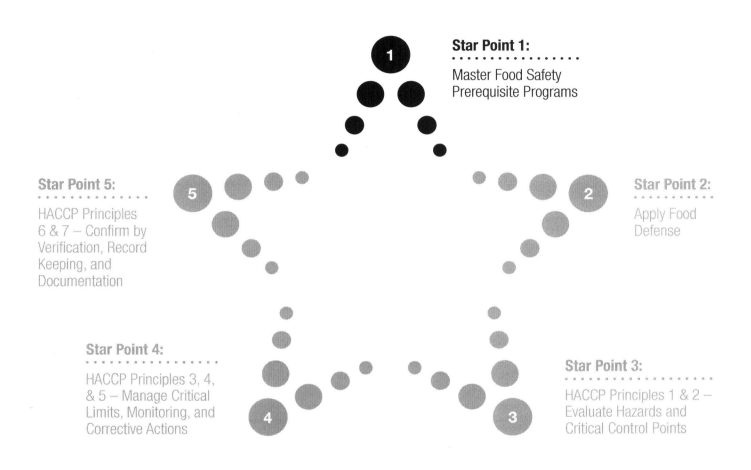

Star Point 1:
Master Food Safety
Prerequisite Programs

Star Point 5:
HACCP Principles
6 & 7 – Confirm by
Verification, Record
Keeping, and
Documentation

Star Point 2:
Apply Food
Defense

Star Point 4:
HACCP Principles 3, 4,
& 5 – Manage Critical
Limits, Monitoring, and
Corrective Actions

Star Point 3:
HACCP Principles 1 & 2 –
Evaluate Hazards and
Critical Control Points

Star Point 1 Myth or Fact (Check one.)

1. Food safety prerequisite programs require food employees to attend college level food safety classes.
____**Myth** ____**Fact**

2. HACCP is a proactive approach to control every step in the flow of food.
____**Myth** ____**Fact**

3. If you prevent a foodborne illness from occurring, then you prevent an outbreak. If you prevent an outbreak, you save lives.
____**Myth** ____**Fact**

4. Hand sanitizers are a good substitute for hand washing for food employees.
____**Myth** ____**Fact**

5. 1 in 3 people do not wash their hands after using the bathroom.
____**Myth** ____**Fact**

Star Point 1 Goals

You will learn to:

- Define HACCP and its goals;
- Identify the causes for foodborne illness;
- Understand how HACCP prevents foodborne illness outbreaks;
- Be prepared to assist customers with food allergies;
- Recognize and understand the importance of Standard Operating Procedures;
- Identify the International Food Safety Icons;
- Apply time and temperatures controls to ensure food safety; and
- Prevent contamination of food.

In Star Point 1, we will discuss the basics of prerequisite programs and food safety standard operating procedures (SOP). We must be aware of how food can become unsafe. We must also have rules and procedures in place to prevent food from becoming unsafe. These rules and procedures are called **prerequisite programs** and **standard operating procedures**. The established food safety actions in prerequisite programs and standard operating procedures are part of all HACCP plans. In order for a HACCP plan to be effective, a good foundation of rules and procedures need to be in place.

Throughout this book, you will be introduced to things that have been identified as the most significant contributing factors to foodborne illness. These are known as **Foodborne Illness Risk Factors**. We know these risk factors, if out of control, will most likely cause someone to get sick. The CDC has identified 5 broad risk factor categories:

    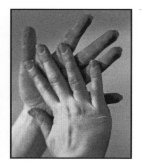

| **Food From Unsafe Sources** | **Inadequate Cooking** | **Improper Holding Temperatures** | **Contaminated Equipment** | **Poor Personal Hygiene** |

You will find, throughout the book, that food safety concepts and HACCP are all connected to one of these 5 basic risk factors.

Understanding and Using Prerequisite Programs and Standard Operating Procedures

Prerequisite programs used in most food service or retail operations relate to food handling and operational activities. These programs include written **standard operating procedures (SOPs)** that clearly define acceptable practices and procedures for the entire establishment and its employees. Prerequisite programs and SOPs must be in place before any food enters an establishment and are required for all HACCP plans. They provide the acceptable practices and procedures that your food service or retail organization requires you to follow. These programs must be explained, demonstrated, and clearly understood by all employees.

An effective HACCP plan will help an operation meet food safety requirements established in the Food Code. Items such as vendor certifications and buyer specifications, training programs for employees, employee understanding of allergen control, written recipes, and other SOPs are all part of the prerequisite programs that are developed by facility owners, operators, and managers.

SOPs are only effective if they are followed! It is important for you to understand that SOPs play a large part in your HACCP plan, the safety of your facility, and the food served. Following and mastering the instructions in the standard operating procedures will ensure the safe flow of food through your food service or retail establishment.

Approved HACCP plans require that each employee follow SOPs at each step in the flow of food. These are standards you must know and practice when you purchase, receive, store, prepare, cook, hold, cool, reheat, and serve food. Job descriptions should make it clear that all employees are expected to follow SOPs. What you do or do not, do as an employee in the food service or retail industry, is important to public health. You can make a difference by following SOPs and by making good decisions that will help keep your customers safe. Your training in food safety could potentially save lives and help raise the quality of food served at your food service or retail establishment. Being **SURE** that you are serving safe food begins with purchase, receive, and proper storage of food.

Purchase Food

Purchasing food from unsafe suppliers is one of the five most common risk factors to food safety according to the CDC. Food must be purchased from legally approved and reputable suppliers that are regulated and inspected to meet compliance standards, including labeling. This helps ensure you are receiving safe food.

As a food employee you may not be involved in the purchasing process, however, you will need to know who your approved suppliers are for receiving purposes. Ask your manager if you are unsure.

Receive Food

Food should be received in sound and safe condition, free from damage, adulteration or contamination. Upon delivery of products purchased from approved suppliers, it is critical to inspect the products properly. Inspecting the delivery can include:

- the vehicle;
- product handling;
- temperature;
- condition; and
- accuracy.

The product must look, feel, and smell right. It's critical that you use your senses. Reject any items that were not ordered or do not meet safe standards. Your manager may have a receiving log for you to fill out verifying product was received properly.

Products and packaging must be received in good condition. Reject items with evidence of:

- Past use-by or sell-by date;
- Damage, tears, rips, dents or rust on cans, and open seals;
- Soiling;
- Stains or leakage;
- Pests being in the product or contaminating it;
- Having been wet;
- Time/temperature abuse; or
- Mislabeling.

Receiving SOP

Purpose: To ensure that all food is received fresh and safe when it enters the food service or retail operation, and to transfer food to proper storage as quickly as possible.

Scope: This procedure applies to food service or retail employees who are responsible for receiving food products into the establishment.

Key Words: Cross contamination, temperatures, receiving, holding, frozen goods, delivery

Instructions:

1. Train food service or retail employees who accept deliveries on proper receiving procedures. These procedures will include actions expected of the trained receiver. The properly trained receiver will only accept food products and supplies from an approved reputable supplier.

2. Schedule deliveries to arrive at designated times during operational hours.

3. Post the delivery schedule, including the names of vendors, days and times of deliveries, and the driver's name.

4. Establish a rejection policy to ensure accurate, timely, consistent, and effective refusal and return of rejected goods.

5. Organize freezer and refrigeration space, loading docks, and store rooms before receiving deliveries.

6. Gather product specification lists and purchase orders, temperature logs, calibrated thermometers, pens, flashlights, and clean loading carts before deliveries.

7. Keep receiving area clean and well lighted.

8. Do not touch RTE foods with bare hands.

9. Determine whether foods will be marked with the date of arrival or the "use by" date and mark accordingly upon receipt.

10. Compare delivery invoice against products ordered and products delivered.

11. Transfer foods to their appropriate locations as quickly as possible.

Monitor: See Star Point 4 HACCP Principle 4

Corrective Action: See Star Point 4 HACCP Principle 5

Verification: See Star Point 5 HACCP Principle 6

Record Keeping/Documentation: See Star Point 5 HACCP Principle 7

Store Food

Storage practices followed in a food operation must ensure that food and products are stored in safe and secure locations and is protected from contamination. Foods may be stored dry (dry storage rooms) or wet (refrigerators or freezers). Common storage practices that ensure that foods are maintained safely include the following:

- Do not store foods in locker rooms, bathrooms, garbage areas, or under unprotected water and sewer lines;
- All storage areas, shelving, and equipment cleaned on a regular basis;
- Food and food related items always kept at least 6 inches (15 cm) off of the floor, away from walls, and protected from contamination;
- All foods labeled with the common name;
- Use-by or sell-by dates clearly included on the label;
- TCS food prepared on site marked with use-by dates not to exceed seven days;
- Frozen foods frozen;
- Cold foods cold: 41°F (5°C) or below;
- Hot foods hot: 135°F (57.2°C) or above;
- Single-use items must be stored in their original packaging;
- Opened and exposed items covered and protected from contamination using food wrap, plastic over-wrap, or lids;
- Dry storage temperatures 50°F - 70°F (10°C - 21.2°C);
- Dry storage relative humidity 50% - 60%; and
- First-in, first-out (FIFO) rotation will ensure that product is used before expiration or use-by date. When new product is received, store it behind products already on the shelves.

Maintaining food product temperature control requires that refrigerators and freezers are working properly. Do not overstock refrigerators or freezers with too much product because it restricts airflow, which can increase food storage temperatures. This could put the food and equipment at risk. When storing raw product in the same cooler, items must be stored properly based on their cooking requirements to minimize cross-contamination. Food items should be stored top to bottom as follows:

- Ready-to-eat food
- Fish, steaks, and chops
- Whole cuts of meat (roasts)
- Ground meat and ground fish
- All poultry

Pop Quiz:
Storage SOP

In the space provided below, complete the instructions needed for a Storage SOP.

Storage SOP

Purpose: To ensure that food is stored safely and put away as quickly as possible after it enters the food service or retail operation.

Scope: This procedure applies to food service or retail employees who handle, prepare, or serve food.

Key Words: Cross contamination, temperatures, storing, dry storage, refrigeration, freezer

Instructions:

1. Freezer temperatures are between _____ .

2. Refrigerator temperatures are between _____ .

3. Dry storage temperatures are between _____ .

4. Dry storage humidity is between _____ .

5. Use a thermometer that is _____ , _____ , _____ .

6. All items are dated upon delivery. Use _____ procedures for rotation.

7. All food must be _____ inches off the floor.

8. TCS foods are stored no more than _____ days at 41°F (5°C) from the date of preparation.

Add your own instructions for storing chemicals and pesticides below for #'s 9 and 10.

9. _____

_____ .

10. _____

_____ .

Understanding Hazards in Food

Standard operating procedures are put in place to control hazards. There are potential hazards in all areas of food service and retail establishments from production through consumption. Hazards fall into three basic categories:

- **Biological Hazards** - (microorganisms) bacteria, viruses, parasites, and fungi. Biological hazards are the greatest threat to food safety and human health.

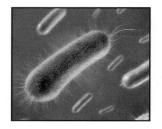  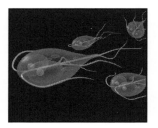 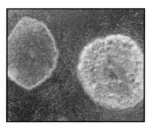

Bacteria   **Viruses**   **Parasites**   **Fungi**

- **Chemical Hazards** - pesticides, unapproved additives or food colors, toxic metals, natural poisons, cleaning chemicals, and similar.

- **Physical Hazards** - hair, dirt, fake fingernails, plastic wrap, band aids, cherry pits, fish bones, and any other object that does not belong in food.

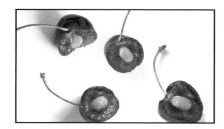 

If you follow your operations SOPs, then you control the hazards. By controlling the hazards, you prevent illness, injury, or even death. As Star Point 1 moves through various SOPs, keep these three hazards in mind.

Basic Microbiology

Biological hazards are of great concern. To understand how to control illness caused by biological hazards, you need to have a basic understanding of how microorganisms (bacteria, viruses, and parasites) live and grow.

Microorganisms are living. All living organisms (bacteria, viruses, and parasites) have basic needs to live, grow and/or multiply/reproduce. Just as we do, microorganisms need **f**ood, controlled **a**cidity, **t**ime, **t**emperature, **o**xygen (or lack thereof) and **m**oisture. This is easy to remember if you can remember **FATTOM**.

FATTOM

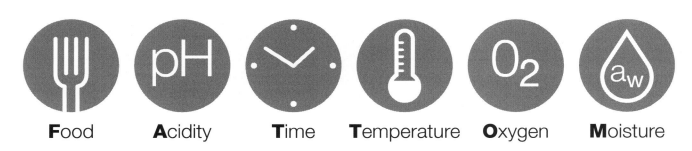

Food   **A**cidity   **T**ime   **T**emperature   **O**xygen   **M**oisture

Generally bacteria thrive in warm, moist, protein-rich, neutral environments. Sound familiar? …it should. This describes a lot of food. To control the growth of germs, you must remove or control the factors that enable them to thrive. Not all bacteria are similar, just like humans. Some like salty environments - some like low oxygen environment. Some like starchy foods and some like high protein foods. If you control **FATTOM**, you control growth, and the threat of illness. You need to put as many barriers in place so that you deny the conditions that support the possible growth of bacteria.

Viruses are the smallest and simplest forms of life. They are little bundles of genetic material that can cause big problems. Viruses will not multiply in food. They need a living host (humans are great hosts). But, they will live and survive in food. The best way to control illness, due to a virus, is by not allowing it to get into food in the first place. The best protection is good personal hygiene.

Parasites are microscopic creatures that need a host to survive. They can travel in food and waste. Once in a human host, they can cause some very unpleasant illnesses. The use of uncontaminated waters, proper cooking, and freezing procedures will destroy most parasites.

Prerequisite programs and SOPs are put into place to control harmful microorganisms from getting into food in the first place, controlling the growth, or destroying those pathogens that may have accidentally gotten into food. SOPs control hazards (biological, chemical, or physical) and prevent illness or injury. Star Point 1 will explore many of these controls.

Understanding Foodborne Illness

If prerequisite programs and SOPs are not followed, you and your customers may contract a foodborne illness. Illnesses that travel to you through food are called **foodborne illnesses**. A foodborne illness is caused by eating food that has been contaminated with a biological or chemical (remember those hazards?) agent that will make you ill once eaten. **Contamination is the unintended, accidental, or deliberate presence of substances or disease causing microorganisms in food.**

A foodborne illness caused by dangerous germs, called **pathogens**, occurs when these pathogens get into your body and make you sick. There are three general categories of foodborne illness.

Foodborne infection – Happens when the bacteria itself makes you sick. The bacteria gives you an infection.

Toxin-mediated infection – Occurs when you consume food with a pathogen in it. While the pathogen is in your body, it produces a toxin (poison). The toxin made by the pathogen *after* you consume it makes you sick.

Foodborne intoxication – The pathogen produces a toxin (poison) in the food before you eat it. You are eating food with a chemical in it. Foodborne illness intoxication can also occur when chemicals accidentally get into food.

A **foodborne illness outbreak** occurs when two or more people eat the same food and get the same illness. Following a HACCP program helps prevent foodborne illness outbreaks because HACCP is a proactive approach to control every step in the flow of food. All the food we eat goes through what we call the flow of food. All flows of food start with the purchasing of food from approved sources. The food is then received, stored, prepared, cooked, held, cooled, reheated, and served, which completes the flow of food. Here are some questions to ask yourself, to determine if you have ever suffered from a foodborne illness:

- Have you ever eaten food that made you sick?
- Did you vomit?
- Did you have stomach cramps?
- Did you have diarrhea?
- Did you ever cough up or pass worms?

Experiencing vomiting, diarrhea, stomach cramps, and flu-like symptoms are the most common symptoms associated with foodborne illnesses. These symptoms could be the result of not following prerequisite programs and SOPs as required by the food service or retail establishment. This chapter should help you to understand food safety so that you can protect yourself, your family, your friends, your neighbors, your fellow employees, and your customers.

Healthy people have immune system antibodies that fight off many of the pathogens that we ingest (daily), but when there are too many germs consumed, germs win the fight and we get sick. There are some people who simply cannot fight off illness as well as healthy people. In the food industry, we call this group of people a **Highly Susceptible Population (HSP)**. If you work in a hospital, nursing home, senior center, daycare, medical treatment or similar, you are serving a HSP. There can be no chances taken with food safety when serving a HSP in a facility of this type. It takes a much lower dose of pathogens to make these people sick.

The people at the most risk for foodborne illness are:

Children

**People already
sick**

**People taking
medication**

**Elderly
people**

**Immune
compromised
persons**

**Persons with
certain diseases**

Did You Know...

Infected employees are the source of contamination of 1 in 5 foodborne illness disease outbreaks reported in the U.S. Most of these are fecal-oral contamination.

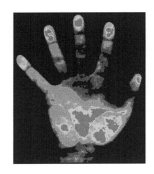

The skin on your hands is very thick and pathogens cannot easily penetrate the skin. A food handler may not get sick from this kind of contact with a pathogen, but the consumer may become violently ill.

Common Foodborne Illnesses

Common foodborne illnesses Hepatitis A, E. coli – scientifically known as Hemorrhagic colitis, Norovirus Infection, Salmonella nontyphoidal, Salmonella typhi (Thyphoid fever), and Shigellosis are some of the most alarming because they are **highly contagious** and **can spread easily**. These illnesses are easily transmitted to others when food handlers do not wash their hands properly after using the restroom or touch RTE foods with bare hands. Spreading disease in this way is called the **fecal-(hand)-oral route**. Keep in mind; these are fecal-(hand)-oral route employee diseases spread person to person. The five highly contagious foodborne illnesses (known as the "**BIG 6**") you need to know:

Hepatitis A (virus)

E. coli – scientifically known Hemorrhagic colitis (bacteria)

Norovirus Infection (virus)

Salmonellosis, i.e. Salmonella nontyphoidal (bacteria)

Salmonella typhi, i.e. Typhoid fever (bacteria)

Shigellosis, i.e. Shigella spp (bacteria)

A good way to remember the Big 6 is simply remember **H.E.N.S.S.S.** Let's review these foodborne illnesses and their most common causes in greater detail. These illnesses are especially crucial to know because they are highly contagious and very serious, sometimes fatal.

Disease	Common Causes
Hepatitis A Virus Infection	Not washing hands properly; infected employee; receiving shellfish from unapproved sources; handling RTE foods, water, and ice with contaminated hands; Highly contagious—**must report** to person-in-charge.
Hemorrhagic colitis (E. coli)	Undercooked ground beef; unpasteurized juice/cider and dairy products; contact with infected animals; and contaminated produce; Highly contagious—**must report** to person-in-charge.
Norovirus Infection	Poor personal hygiene, receiving shellfish from unapproved sources and using unsanitary/non-chlorinated water; Easily passed among people in close quarters for long periods of time (dormitories, offices, and cruise ships); Highly contagious—**must report** to person-in-charge.
Salmonellosis (*Salmonella* nontyphoidal, NTS)	Ingesting contaminated food such as beef, eggs, poultry, unpasteurized milk, or water. Food can be contaminated by an infected food handler. Highly contagious—**must report** to person-in-charge.s
Typhoid fever (*Salmonella typhi*)	Ingesting contaminated water or eating raw fruits and vegetables that have been washed or irrigated with contaminated water. Highly contagious—**must report** to person-in-charge.
Shigellosis (Shigella spp., Dysentery, Bacillary Dysentery)	Flies, water, and foods contaminated with fecal matter; Highly contagious—**must report** to person-in-charge.

Did You Know...

In most cases, you do not get ill immediately from consuming food contaminated with any of the Big 6 or similar pathogens. It can take 30 minutes or up to 30 days for you to begin showing signs of illness depending on the pathogen. The average time is 2 – 24 hours after the food is eaten. This is called the incubation period. Foods containing toxins will cause illness very quickly, within seconds in some cases.

Common Diseases from Foods

Bacteria	Virus	Parasite
Bacillus Cereus Gastroenteritis	**Hepatitis A Virus Infection***	Anisakiasis
Botulism	**Norovirus Infection***	Cryptosporidiosis
Campylobacteriosis	Rotavirus Gastroenteritis	Cyclosporiasis
Clostridium perfringens Gastroenteritis		Giardiasis
Hemorrhagic colitis (E. coli)*		Toxoplasmosis
Listeriosis		Trichinosis
Salmonella (nontyphoidal)*		
Salmonella typhi (Typhod fever)*		
Shigellosis (Bacillary Dysentery)*		
Staphylococcal Gastroenteritis		
Vibrio Infection		
Yersiniosis		

The highlighted items above indicate the BIG 6 foodborne illnesses.

Following prerequisite programs and SOPs will help to prevent diseases like these from occurring or spreading. **If you prevent a foodborne illness from occurring, then you prevent an outbreak. If you prevent an outbreak, you save lives.** If you save lives, you can feel good about what you do for a living and ultimately protect others—and yourself.

Pop Quiz:

Fill in the blanks to identify the Big 6 foodborne illness causing pathogens

H = _____   S = _____

E = _____   S = _____

N = _____   S = _____

Major Food Allergens

Some of the symptoms associated with a foodborne illness are the same symptoms associated with an allergic reaction. When it comes to food safety, food allergies are just as dangerous as foodborne illnesses. The food code requires that employees are trained in allergy awareness. Ask your manager if your company has an SOP to identify allergens on the menu and control them within the facility. Employees should have a general understanding of allergens, but ultimately if you are not sure, always ask the Person-in-Charge (PIC). Never give your customers an answer as to what is in the food unless you are sure. The wrong answer could be deadly! The PIC is required to have a working understanding of allergens and allergen control. As another preventative measure for allergen control, the Food Code now requires that equipment and utensils that come into contact with a major raw animal food allergen, such as fish, and that will be followed by other types of raw animal foods will need to be cleaned and sanitized first before moving onto the other types of raw animal foods.

Is your customer having an allergic reaction to food? Let's find out. . .

- Is your customer's throat getting tight?
- Does your customer have shortness of breath?
- Does your customer have itching around the mouth?
- Does your customer have hives?

Any food item can potentially cause an allergic reaction. Sometimes people do not know they have a food allergy until they have a reaction to a food that causes some of the symptoms listed. This is in the prerequisite programs point of the HACCP Star because allergies are a growing concern in the effort to serve and sell safe food. The Food Code now includes Allergens as a natural chemical hazard (if not identified properly).

If you are or know of someone who has had an allergic reaction to food, you can understand how important it is to know what is in the foods you, your family, friends, neighbors, fellow employees, and customers are consuming. The first step is to be aware of the most common allergens. Although there are others, the most common, known as Major Food Allergens or the "**Big 8**," are:

| Milk (dairy products) | Eggs | Soy/tofu | Wheat |

| Tree Nuts | Peanuts | Fish (bass, flounder, or cod, etc.) | Crustacean Shellfish (crab, lobster, or shrimp, etc.) |

Copyright © International Association for Food Protection

What are Tree Nuts?

- Almond
- Brazil Nut
- Cashew
- Chestnut
- Coconut
- Hazelnut

- Hickory Nut
- Macadamia Nut
- Pecan
- Pine Nut
- Pistachio
- Walnut

Some allergens cause reactions that range from mild to severe enough to cause death. You should take the following steps to ensure your customers avoid eating foods to which they are allergic. First, think about how you would like to be treated if you were the customer with a food allergy. Then consider the following steps:

1. **Know your menu.** Describe all ingredients and the preparation of foods you are serving to anyone who asks, even if it is a "secret recipe." No one is asking for the specifics on how to make a secret recipe, just what ingredients are in it. You MUST provide this information to your customers. Be aware of all ingredients in food products used to make a menu item.

2. **Be honest.** It is OK to say, "I don't know." Immediately ask your manager to assist you. Remember the PIC is the resident expert.

3. **Know your company's SOP.** What should you do if your customer indicates that they have a food allergy?

4. **Ask your customers** if anyone has any food allergies.

5. **Be careful.** Make sure your customer is not allergic to anything in the food you are serving. You should also make certain that this person is not allergic to anything with which the food has come into contact (SOP: Prevent Cross-Contamination). For example, the entrée they ordered may not contain peanuts, but your facility does have peanuts in the kitchen. Be careful not to cross contaminate!

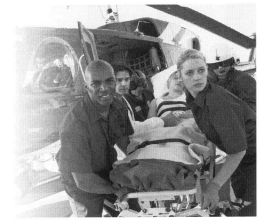

6. **Be thoughtful and concerned**, but never tell a customer you are sorry this person has an allergy to certain foods, because no one is at fault for having the allergy.

7. **Manage allergens by limiting the contact** of the food of concern for any allergic customer. It is best if only 1 person handles the customer's entire food preparation and service. Even utensils and plates can cause cross contamination of allergens to several surfaces.

If a customer has an allergic reaction at your food service or retail establishment then seek immediate medical treatment. Every second counts!

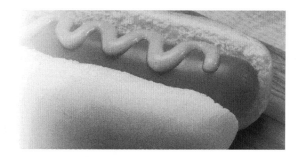

Star Knowledge Exercise:

Foodborne Illness & Allergens

How well do you understand foodborne illnesses and food allergens? Answer the following questions:

1. If you have been diagnosed with or come in contact with someone who has Hepatitis A, what should you do? (Circle the correct letter.)

a. Notify the Person-in-Charge.

b. Continue to work because you are under a doctor's care.

c. Wash hands more often.

2. Check the "BIG 6" foodborne illnesses.

_____ Trichinosis		_____ Norovirus
_____ Botulism		_____ Salmonella typhi
_____ Hepatitis A		_____ Vibrio Infection
_____ E. coli		_____ Anisakiasis
_____ Listeriosis		_____ Shigellosis

3. How would you handle a customer who tells you they are allergic to walnuts, but wants to order the chicken salad that has toasted walnuts in it? (Circle the correct letter.)

a. It is not my responsibility. It is the customer's responsibility to make the right decision.

b. Using a gloved hand, remove the walnuts before serving the salad.

c. Recommend a different food item that does not contain walnuts.

4. Check the "BIG 8" major food allergens.

_____ Peanuts	_____ Tomatoes	_____ Eggs
_____ Cherries	_____ Crustacean Shellfish	_____ Melons
_____ Soy/Tofu	_____ Beef	_____ Milk (dairy products)
_____ Poultry	_____ Wheat	_____ Tree Nuts
_____ Sugar	_____ Fish	_____ Salt

5. A_____ occurs when two or more people eat the same food and get the same illness. (Circle the correct letter.)

a. foodborne intoxication

b. foodborne infection

c. foodborne illness outbreak

Track Your Action Items

International Food Safety Icons

We all know what the blue handicapped parking sign means when we drive through a parking lot. Signs with simple pictures tell us when it is safe to cross the street, when to check the oil in our car, and how to get to the airport. With the same purpose in mind, International Food Safety Icons help to make food safety easier for everyone to understand and help you to remember basic food safety rules and procedures for food preparation. Throughout this section, you will see the various International Food Safety Icons, which will help you succeed in becoming a HACCP All-Star. The International Food Safety Icons provide a visual definition and reminder of the Standard Operating Procedures for the food service or retail industry. A team of managers and supervisors has established prerequisite programs, policies, procedures, and recipes that must be followed. The International Food Safety Icons make it easy to understand, remember, and reinforce these procedures.

Pop Quiz:

Food Safety Match Game

Complete the following exercise by matching the letter from the International Food Safety Icons with the phrase that best describes the icon.

1. _____ Do Not Work If Ill
2. _____ Cold Holding—Hold cold foods below 41°F (5°C)
3. _____ No Bare-Hand Contact—Do not handle food with bare hands
4. _____ Hot Holding—Hold hot foods above 135°F (57.2°C)
5. _____ Temperature Danger Zone (TDZ)—41°F to 135°F (5°C to 57.2°C)
6. _____ Time/Temperature Control for Safety of Food (TCS)
7. _____ Cook All Foods Thoroughly
8. _____ Wash Your Hands
9. _____ Do Not Cross Contaminate—between raw to RTE or cooked foods
10. _____ Wash, Rinse, Sanitize
11. _____ Cooling Food

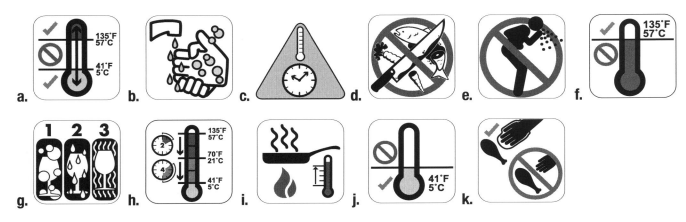

Copyright © International Association for Food Protection

How many points did you earn? _____

If you scored 10–11 points—Congratulations! You are a Food Safety All-Star!

If you scored 8–9 points—Good job! You have a basic understanding of food safety.

If you scored 5–7 points—The time for review is now! What a great opportunity to fine-tune your food safety skills.

If you scored 0–4 points—Everyone needs to start somewhere!

Employee Responsibilities Related to Food Safety

As an employee, some of your personal responsibilities related to providing safe food includes; staying home when sick, washing your hands, using gloves properly, and following a food-safe dress code. Each International Food Safety Icon represents a food safety standard operating procedure. Let's explore those relating to employee health and hygiene.

Do Not Work If Ill

Did you know that the Food Code actually requires that employees report contact with or exposed to certain illnesses to their employer? It also requires that employees report to the **Person-In-Charge (PIC)** – usually a manager or owner – if they are experiencing certain signs and symptoms.

An employee must report to the PIC if they have any of the following symptoms:

- Vomiting;
- Diarrhea;
- Jaundice (unnatural yellowing of the eyes or skin);
- Sore throat with fever; or
- Lesions containing pus or an infected wound that is open and draining on the arms or hands.

> What do you do about a common cold? Or seasonal allergies? If you are sure that you only have a common cold or an allergy, and are not experiencing any of the above listed symptoms you can typically report to work. Always check with your manager to discuss your work for the day. Your PIC will most likely assign you to a duty that has the least exposure to food. No one wants someone sneezing all over their food! Your management might have a much stricter SOP for any kind of sniffling, sneezing, or cold type symptoms. Though colds (and seasonal flu) do not cause foodborne illness, they are easily transmitted through the air and surfaces to other people. You do not want to be the cause of making the entire staff sick. Staying home and resting is always the best answer.

A food employee must also report to the PIC:

- If they are currently diagnosed with any of the Big 6;
- Lives with or has been in close contact with someone who has, has been exposed to, or has been potentially exposed to the Big 6;
- Have had an illness in the past 3 months and diagnosed as *Salmonella typhi* (Typhoid fever); or
- Have been exposed to or is a suspected source of a confirmed foodborne illness outbreak.

The PIC in the food facility will make a determination, based on their knowledge of the Food Code and guidance from their regulatory agency, whether you can report work, with or without restriction, or if you must be excluded all together from coming to work unless you have been seen by a Health Practitioner.

Remember, as soon as you find out you have been exposed to or have contracted any of these illnesses, notify your manager immediately! The Big 6 illness must be reported to the regulatory agency. You will not get in trouble for telling...you will be saving lives!

Wash Your Hands

Washing your hands frequently is extremely important in preventing illness. Wash your hands! Wash your hands! Wash your hands!

Use the following hand washing recipe:

1. If the paper towel dispenser requires you to touch the handle or lever, the first step should be to crank down the paper towel. Let the paper towel hang there. Do not do this if the paper towel touches and cross contaminates with the wall or the waste container.

2. Wet your hands using water that is 100°F (37.8°C)

3. Add soap

4. Scrub for 20 seconds
   - Do not forget your nails, thumbs, and between your fingers
   - Some regulators require nailbrushes

5. Rinse

6. Dry with a clean paper towel

After exiting a restroom, wash your hands again when you re-enter the kitchen! Did you know that 33% of people do not wash their hands after using the restroom? Guess what they touch when they leave the restroom? Everything, including the door handles. So always wash your hands when you re-enter the kitchen or before you do any activity that requires you to handle food or food contact surfaces.

When do you wash your hands and change your gloves?

- After going to the bathroom (fecal-(hand)-oral route)
- Before and after food preparation
- After touching your hair, face, or any other body parts
- After scratching your scalp
- After rubbing your ear
- After touching a pimple
- After wiping your nose and using a tissue
- After sneezing and coughing into your hand
- After drinking, eating, or smoking
- After touching your apron or uniform

- After touching the telephone or door handle
- After touching raw food and before touching RTE products
- After cleaning and handling all chemicals
- After taking out the trash
- After touching any non-food contact surfaces
- Every 4 hours during constant use
- After touching a pen
- After handling money
- After receiving deliveries
- Before starting your shift

Did You Know...
- Hand sanitizers should only be used on clean hands.
- Hand sanitizers are not a substitute for hand washing in the food service or retail industry.
- You should only use sanitizers approved by the FDA.

No Bare-Hand Contact

You must not touch Ready-To-Eat (RTE) foods with bare hands. RTE foods are exactly that: ready-to-eat such as bread, pickles, lunchmeats, cherries, lettuce, lemon wedges, cheese,…and yes, sushi too. These foods should be handled with gloves, deli paper, tongs, or utensils. Why? Even a good thorough hand washing does not get rid of all bad germs on your hands. No bare-hand contact with RTE food is another precaution to avoid foodborne illness. Remember, one in three people do not wash their hands after using the bathroom. For these reasons, there is **no bare-hand contact with RTE food**. It stops the fecal-(hand)-oral route of contamination.

Your food facility should have an SOP for glove use. Follow that SOP exactly. Gloves are not worn to keep your hands from getting messy. Gloved hands assure that any germs on your hands, even after a good handwashing, are kept away from foods. Gloves are an extension of your hands. If they get contaminated, they must be changed. Even if not contaminated, they should be changed at least every 4 hours. If glove use is not an SOP for your facility, the Food Code still requires that you not touch RTE foods with your bare hands.

If a RTE food is going to be added as an ingredient to a food item that will be fully cooked, like a topping for a pizza or adding vegetables to a casserole, bare-hand contact is not required prior to the cook step. Once cooked, hands off! This would not apply if the food will only be lightly heated, melted, browned, or otherwise undercooked.

Do you have to wear gloves when washing raw, whole fruits, and vegetable? No. The Food Code does allow for fruit and vegetables to be handled with bare hands only during the washing step. However, employees must be sure to properly wash their hands prior to washing the fruit and vegetables.

Did You Know...

Pre-cut or prewashed produce in bags should not be washed before use. Pre-cut bagged produce items are considered a RTE food and should not be touched with bare hands.

Pop Quiz:
True or False

1. You can touch a piece of toast with your bare hands. **True / False**

2. You can use your hands to place tomatoes and onion in your uncooked casserole. **True / False**

3. After washing, raw fruits and vegetable may be touched with bare hands. **True / False**

Cross Contamination

Between Raw and RTE or Cooked Foods

 Raw food is food that needs to be cooked before eaten, like raw meat and eggs. RTE food is food that doesn't need to be cooked and is ready to be eaten, like bread or lettuce. Cooked food is food that has been properly cooked by reaching a specific temperature for an appropriate amount of time, like a cooked hamburger. Once food has been properly cooked, it is now considered RTE food.

Food Contact Surfaces

Cross contamination occurs when raw food touches or shares contact with RTE and/or cooked foods. Touching the walk-in (refrigerator/cooler) door handle, or a pen, or the telephone, and then making a sandwich, without putting on new gloves is cross contamination. Cross contamination occurs when the same knife is used to cut both raw chicken and bread. If raw chicken is stored in the refrigerator above lettuce and the chicken drips onto the lettuce, this is cross contamination.

To avoid cross contamination:

- Properly store raw food below RTE food (raw chicken below lettuce);
- Properly clean and sanitize utensils, equipment, and surfaces;
- Clean and sanitize work areas when changing from raw food preparation to RTE food preparation; and
- Wash your hands between all tasks and any time they may have been contaminated.

Between Tasks

It is critical to change gloves, wash hands, use clean and sanitized utensils, cutting boards, and work surfaces between tasks to prevent contamination. Here are some ways to place a barrier between you and cross contamination. Use different colored gloves for different jobs. This system makes it easy to separate food-handling jobs from non-food-handling jobs. Ask your manager if your company has a SOP for gloves. Here are some examples of color coding gloves:

- Use clear gloves for food preparation.
- Use blue gloves for fish.
- Use yellow gloves for poultry.
- Use red gloves for beef.
- Use purple gloves for cleaning and non-food contact surfaces.

Designate different cloths and containers and code them to separate food and non-food contact surfaces. For example:

- Use a white cloth for food contact surfaces.
- Use a blue cloth for non-food-contact surfaces.
- Use a green container for cleaning (water and soap).
- Use a red container for sanitizing (water and sanitizer).
- Use color coded cutting boards, knives, containers, and gloves.

Dress Code

Follow these rules to avoid violating the dress code:

- Cover all cuts and burns with a bandage and a glove.
- Wear a hat or other proper hair restraint (the shift manager and managers who are exposed to or come in close contact with food must wear a hair restraint).
- Wear a neat and clean uniform and apron.
- Wear clean, closed-toe shoes with rubber soles.
- Take a bath or shower every day.
- Always have clean and neat hair.
- Properly groom fingernails and hands.
- Do not wear nail polish or false nails.
- Do not wear rings, watches, and bracelets.
- According to the Food Code the only exception is a plain wedding band.
- A medical alert necklace can be tucked under the shirt or a medical alert ankle bracelet can be worn.

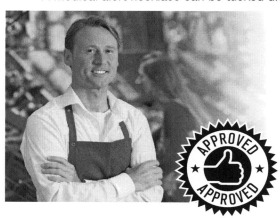

- As an extra precaution, do not wear necklaces, dangly or hoop earrings, or facial piercings, especially if they could fall or drop into food and cause a physical hazard.
- Do not chew gum.
- Only eat, drink, and smoke in designated areas.
- Do not touch your hair, your face, or any other body parts when handling or serving food.
- Remove aprons before leaving the food preparation areas.
- Wear a clean apron and uniform at all times.
- Never take your apron into the bathroom.

Sampling Food

Cross contamination can occur when sampling food at your workstation. You should never eat at your workstation unless you are taste-testing food you are preparing.

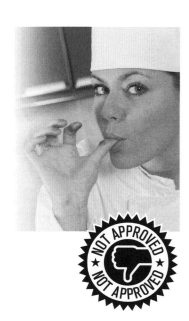

- Use a single-use spoon. Do not double dip! Single-use means exactly that—only one taste per single-use spoon. Or take a small dish; ladle a small portion of the food into the small dish. Put down the ladle. Step away from the pan or pot. Then taste the food. Place items in the dirty dish area of your establishment.
- Always wash your hands properly and return to work.

Time/Temperature Control For Safety of Food (TCS)

A **time/temperature control for safety of food (TCS)** is any food capable of allowing bacteria to grow or form toxins. These TCS foods have the potential to cause foodborne illness outbreaks. Pathogens love TCS foods. They are usually moist (like watermelon), have lots of protein (like dairy and meat), and do not have very high or very low acidity (neutral acidity). Adding lemon juice or vinegar to foods to increase the acidity can slow the growth of the germs. Remember FATTOM? When trying to control a pathogen from growing, one of the things you need to control is **Time and Temperature**. It is the most common and easily achieved control measure in the food service and retail food setting.

TCS food requires strict time and temperature controls to stay safe. Food has been time–temperature abused anytime it has been in the **temperature danger zone (TDZ)** which is between 41°F - 135°C (5°C -57.2°C) for too long (4 hours). TCS foods must be checked often to make sure that they stay safe. The caution sign includes a clock and thermometer to stress the importance of monitoring time and temperature. The clock is the reminder to check food at regular time intervals (like every 2 or 4 hours). The thermometer required must be properly calibrated, cleaned, and sanitized after each use.

Here is a list of time/temperature control for safety of foods (TCS):

- Cut tomatoes (sliced/diced)
- Mixtures with cut tomatoes (tossed salad, Gazpacho soup)
- Cut leafy greens (lettuce, spinach, cabbage, kale, escarole, endive, spring mix, arugula, and chard)
- Milk and milk products
- Shell eggs
- Fish
- Poultry
- Shellfish and crustaceans
- Meats: beef, pork, and lamb

- Baked or boiled potatoes
- Cooked rice, beans, and pastas
- Heat-treated plant food (cooked vegetables)
- Garlic-and-oil mixtures
- Sprouts/sprout seeds
- Sliced melons
- Tofu and other soy-protein food
- Synthetic ingredients (i.e., soy in meat alternatives)
- Most moist baked goods

These foods require **time/temperature control for safety of food (TCS)** because of their moisture, protein, and acidity characteristics. Remember FATTOM?

Here is a list of some **Non-TCS** foods:

- A loaf of bread (low moisture)
- Lemon wedges (acidic)
- Pickles (acidic)
- Dry Cereals (low moisture)
- Some, but not all, fruit pies (low moisture and/or acidic)

- Jelly/Jams (high sugar)
- Mustard (acidic)
- Chocolate chip cookies (low moisture)

Notice these are very dry, very sugary, or very acidic. Remember FATTOM? Non-TCS food all have barriers to keep pathogens from growing.

Pop Quiz:

Which of the following are conditions that pathogens on TCS foods *generally* like? (Circle any that apply.)

1. High in protein

2. Lots of sugar

3. Lots of acid (pH 3.0)

4. Neutral acidity

5. Fat

6. Hot temperatures (Above 135°F)

7. Salt

8. Moisture

Temperature Danger Zone (TDZ)

Be Safe—Monitor Time and Temperature!

This symbol means no food should stay between **41°F and 135°F** (5°C–57.2°C), as this is the **temperature danger zone (TDZ)**. Germs and bacteria grow and multiply very, very fast in this zone. If a TCS stays in the temperature danger zone for more than 4 hours, it is time–temperature abused and can make people very sick. It is important to practice temperature control (TC) to make sure foods are not time–temperature abused. In the Food Code, there is an exception to the 4 hour rule. If the internal temperature of food is 41°F (5°C) or lower, once it is removed from TC cold holding it can remain out of TC for up to 6 hours as long as the internal product temperature does not go above 70°F.

Since foods should not sit on the counter for more than 4 accumulated hours, you should put food away as soon as possible. You should also check holding units (ovens/refrigerators/freezers/warmers/serving lines) at regular intervals to ensure food safety. For example, if the steam table was accidentally unplugged, it could result in the food temperature dropping to 120°F (48.9°C). If the last time you took the temperature of the food on the table was less than 4 hours ago, you can reheat the food to 165°F (73.9°C) for 15 seconds within 2 hours and continue to serve the product. But if the last time you took the temperature was more than 4 hours ago, then you MUST discard all the foods that are time–temperature abused. This unsafe food can make anyone who eats it sick.

Something to think about…What is the temperature of a healthy human?

If you answered 98.6°F (37°C) you are correct. 98.6°F (37°C) is right in the middle of the temperature danger zone. Our bodies are ideal for germs because we are in the TDZ! Germs love people! Those germs will be transferred to people's food if you are not careful. That is why controlling time and temperature along with maintaining good personal hygiene are keys to the success of food safety.

Checking Food Temperatures with Calibrated Thermometers

What is the point of checking temperatures if you have no clue whether the thermometer is working properly? Calibrated thermometers ensure that the temperatures being read reflect the true temperature of the food. When minimum internal temperatures are achieved the pathogens are reduced or eliminated to a safe level! There are many types of thermometers; bimetallic, thermocouple, infrared with probe, digital, and disposable temperature indicators to name a few. Thermometers must be checked every shift for correct calibration. The simple act of dropping a thermometer on the floor or banging the thermometer against a prep table can knock the thermometer out of calibration. All food must be checked with a properly calibrated, cleaned, and sanitized thermometer. Remember, to avoid cross contamination; clean and sanitize the thermometer before each task change!

Ice-Point Method

  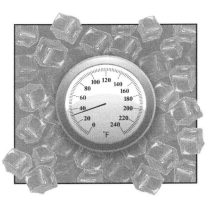

Step 1: Fill a container with crushed ice and water

Step 2: Submerge sensing area of stem or probe for 30 seconds or until indicator needle stops moving

Step 3: Hold calibration nut and rotate thermometer head until it reads 32°F (0°C)

Boiling-Point Method

  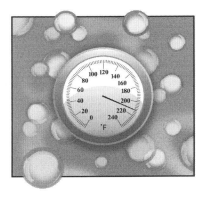

Step 1: Bring a deep pan of water to a boil

Step 2: Submerge sensing area of stem or probe for 30 seconds or until indicator needle stops moving

Step 3: Hold calibration nut and rotate thermometer head until it reads 212ºF (100ºC) at sea level

Note: Follow the manufacturer's procedures for calibrating thermometers. Ask your manager to show you this procedure.

Did You Know...

You cannot thaw foods:

- Using a dishwasher
- In an electric blanket
- In a bath tub
- On a countertop

Properly Thaw Foods

Often we need to thaw food prior to starting the cooking process. How many times have you thought, "We can pull the turkeys from the freezer and let them sit on the work table to thaw?" Setting frozen food on the counter to thaw is not a safe food handling practice. Food should not enter the TDZ to thaw. If it does enter the TDZ it needs to be done in a safe and controlled way.

There are four safe and approved methods for thawing food:

Method 1: Thaw in the refrigerator.
As foods thaw they may produce extra liquid. Be sure to place TCS in a refrigerator, in a pan or on a tray to avoid cross contamination. You must plan ahead to thaw. Larger and denser food items might take several days to thaw in the refrigerator.

Method 2: Thaw in running water.
Foods to be thawed under **running water** must be placed in a sink with running water at 70°F (21.1°C) or cooler. The sink must be open to allow the water to push the microorganisms off the food and flow down the drain. Do not allow the sink to fill with water. Also, **do not allow food to exceed 41°F (5°C) for more than 4 hours total time**.

Method 3: Cooking. Frozen food can be thawed by following the cooking directions for the product. Frozen food may take longer to cook depending on the size and type of product.

Method 4: Microwave. Food can be thawed using the microwave only if it will then be immediately cooked. When thawing food in the microwave, remember that there will be uneven thawing and some of the food may have started to cook, taking some of the food into the TDZ. This is why you must finish the cooking process immediately after microwave thawing.

Cook All Foods Thoroughly

 Each TCS food has a minimum internal cooking temperature that must be reached and held for a specified amount of time at that temperature to ensure that it is safe and less likely to make anyone sick. These safe cooking temperatures will assure that most harmful bacteria or viruses are killed or reduced to harmless levels. Foods known to cause serious illness or death such as eggs and ground meats must be monitored routinely for proper cooking temperatures with a properly cleaned, sanitized, and calibrated thermometer.

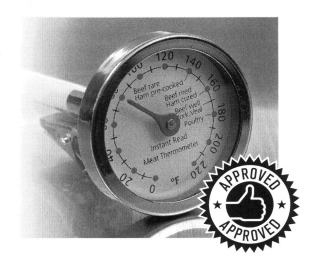

The only way to tell if food is properly cooked is by checking it with a calibrated thermometer. Don't rely on look, touch, or color to determine doneness.

Minimum Internal Cooking Temperatures

Here are some minimum internal cooking temperatures to keep in mind when preparing food:

165°F (73.9°C) for < 1 second

- Reheat all leftover foods.
- Cook all poultry.
- Cook all stuffed products, including pasta.
- Raw animal foods cooked in a microwave, then let sit for 2 minutes.
- When combining already cooked and raw TCS products (casseroles).
- Cook all wild game animals.
- Cook all raw animal foods that have been partially cooked (no longer than 60 minutes and properly cooled).

155°F (68.3°C) for 17 Seconds or 158°F for < 1 second

Note: Check with your Manager

- Cook all ground animal foods: fish, beef, commercially raised game animals, ratites (emu, ostrich, and rhea), and pork.
- Cook all flavor-injected meats.
- Cook all eggs for hot holding and later service (buffet service).

145°F (62.8°C) for 15 Seconds

- Cook all fish and shellfish.
- Cook all intact meat such as chops/steaks of veal, beef, pork, commercially raised game animals, and lamb.
- Cook fresh eggs and egg products for immediate service. (cooked to order)
- Cook roasts to 145°F for 4 minutes. (Roasting temperatures vary, see your manager for the proper procedure in your establishment.)

135°F (57.2°C)

- Reheating processed products for hot holding.
- Cooking vegetables and fruits for hot holding.

Hot Holding

Here are time and temperature food safety rules for hot holding of foods:

- All foods must be cooked before being placed in hot holding units.
- Store all hot food in hot holding/self-service bars (steam table) above 135°F (57.2°C).
- Check temperatures of the food in hot holding a minimum of every 4 hours with a calibrated, cleaned, and sanitized thermometer.
- Always keep food out of the TDZ.

Cold Holding

Here are time and temperature food safety rules for cold holding of foods:

- In cold holding/self-service bars (refrigeration), store all cold food below 41°F (5°C).
- Check temperatures of the food in cold holding a minimum of every 4 hours with a calibrated, cleaned, and sanitized thermometer.
- Always keep food out of the TDZ.

Time as a Public Health Control

The Food Code does allow for the safety of food to be controlled by time instead of temperature. This is called 'time as a public health control'. Bacteria grow if they are in the TDZ for too long. If you cannot control the temperature of the food, you can control the amount of time the food does not have TC. There must be a written and approved procedure in the facility to use time as a public health control.

- **Hot Foods** – If the internal temperature of hot food is 135°F (57.2°C) or higher, once it is removed from TC, hot food can remain out of temperature for up to 4 hours before being consumed or discarded. Your manager should have an approved written plan that details how this process is to be controlled and monitored. Remember, it must be <u>eaten or thrown out after 4 hours</u>.
- **Cold Foods** – If the internal temperature of cold food is 41°F (5°C) or lower, once it is removed from TC, cold food can remain out of temperature for up to 4 hours before being consumed or discarded. Your manager should have an approved written plan that details how this process is to be controlled and monitored. Remember, it must be <u>eaten or thrown out after 4 hours</u>.
- **Cold Foods kept below 70°F (21.1°C)** – If the internal temperature of food is 41°F (5°C) or lower, once it is removed from TC it can remain out of temperature for up to 6 hours as long as the internal temperature does not go above 70°F (21.1°C). There must be a written procedure in place. Ask you manager to review this procedure. Again, it must be <u>eaten or thrown out after 6 hours</u>.

Cooling Food

Two-stage cooling allows TCS food to be in the temperature danger zone for more than 4 hours only if these strict guidelines are followed. Cool hot food from:

135°F to 70°F (57.2°C to 21.1°C) within 2 hours; you then have an additional 4 hours to go from 70°F to 41°F (21.1°C to 5°C) or lower for a <u>maximum total cool time of 6 hours</u>.

Cool food as quickly as possible. Keep in mind, **6 hours is the maximum amount of time, but only if you reach 70°F (21.1°C) within 2 hours**. This additional 4 hours is because the food moves through the most dangerous section of the TDZ within the first two hours. Less time is better Your goal when cooling food is to move food as quickly as possible through the TDZ.

If the food does not reach 70°F (21.1°C) within 2 hours, you must either discard the food or immediately reheat it to 165°F (73.9°C) and begin the cooling process again from that point.

Food cooled from room temperature (ambient, approximately ~70°F (21.1°C) has a 4 hour cool time. An example is a can of tuna removed from dry storage used to make tuna salad. Once opened, you have 4 hours to bring the tuna/tuna salad down to below 41°F (5°C).

Did You Know...

Food must cool from above 135°F (57.2°C) to 70°F (21.1°C) in 2 hours otherwise harmful bacteria might grow.

Proper ways to cool food quickly

- Use a clean and sanitized ice paddle.
- Stir food to release the heat.
- Use an ice bath.
- Add ice as an ingredient.
- Use a quick-chill unit such as a blast chiller.
- Separate food into smaller portions or thinner pieces.

Pop Quiz:
Matching Game

1. _____ Cold Holding Food

2. _____ Hot Food Time as a Public Health Control

3. _____ Cooling Food

4. _____ Cold Food Time as a Public Health Control

5. _____ Hot Food Holding

a. 135ºF to 70ºF (57.2ºC to 21.1ºC) within two hours; then 70ºF to 41ºF (21.1ºC to 5ºC) or lower within four hours

b. 135ºF (57.2ºC) or above

c. 135ºF (57.2ºC) or above (then removed from heat) for up to four hours, then discard

d. 41ºF (5ºC) or below

e. 41ºF (5ºC) or below, (then removed from cold) for up to six hours, as long as the food does not go above 70ºF (21.1ºC), then discard

Once food has cooled to 70°F (21.1°C), it should be placed in the refrigerator as follows.

- Place food in shallow stainless steel pans (no more than 4 inches deep).
- Make sure the pan cover is loose to allow the heat to escape.
- Place pans on top shelves in refrigeration units.
- Position pans so air circulates around them. (Be cautious not to overload refrigerator tray racks.)
- Monitor food to ensure cooling to 41°F (5°C) or lower occurs as quickly as possible so as not to exceed the two-stage cooling process.

The warmest food that can be placed in a refrigerator is 70°F (21.1°C); in a freezer, 41°F (5°C). If hot food is placed in a refrigerator or freezer it will cause the equipment to work harder to cool the food. Also, the warm food will cause the temperature and any refrigerated or frozen food that is already stored there to rise. When this happens the temperature of the properly stored food may rise into the temperature danger zone (TDZ). By taking this dangerous action one risks foodborne illness, ruining the food, and may damage the refrigerator or freezer.

Reheating

The goal of reheating is to move food as quickly as possible through the TDZ. It is critical when reheating food for hot holding to reach a **minimum of 165°F (73.9°C) for 15 seconds within 2 hours**. If food takes longer than 2 hours to reheat (bring to the required internal temperature), it must be discarded or thrown away. Use steam when possible to reheat food and not dry heat. Never use hot holding equipment to reheat (or cook) food, because the equipment is not designed to heat food rapidly.

Commercially prepared, hermetically sealed foods and foods in un-opened packages from food processing plants that are RTE are considered cooked unless the label has cooking instructions. An example of this would be canned soup or frozen RTE chicken patties. If being reheated for hot holding, these types of food must be reheated to 135°F (57.2°C) or above within 2 hours and hot held at 135°F (57.2°C) or above.

For Reheating Food

Foods that are being reheated and **not hot held** (reheated to a customer's request) can be reheated (warmed) and served at any temperature. Only foods that will be hot held must be rapidly reheated before they are placed in hot holding units. You can take a cold pizza out of your refrigerator the next morning and eat it cold right away. If you want to warm up the pizza and keep it in the oven until your friends come over at lunchtime, then you need to reheat it to **165°F (73.9°C) for 15 seconds within 2 hours**.

Cleaning and Sanitizing Food Contact Surfaces and Equipment

Wash, Rinse, Sanitize

Clean and Sanitize! "Sparkle"

Follow Proper Cleaning and Sanitizing Food Safety Rules

What is Cleaning?

Cleaning is removing the dirt or soil on a surface. It is critical you look at what you clean. The expectation is for everything to "sparkle!" A sparkling-clean food service or retail operation impresses every customer. Using approved cleaners, clean all surfaces, equipment, and utensils every 4 hours or when they become soiled or no longer "sparkle." You can use appropriate detergents or solvents or scraping to clean. Unclean table tops and dishes make customers very unhappy. Even if they do not say anything to you about what they found, it leaves a bad impression and they may not return.

Follow the company SOP on cleaning and cleaning chemicals. Do not use a chemical on a food contact surface that is not approved for food contact surfaces in food facilities. If you run out of cleaner, talk with the PIC for alternative chemicals. Some cleaners are not approved to be in contact with food and could make someone ill if used (chemical poisoning). Never substitute a chemical if you are unsure if it will be safe.

What Does It Mean to Sanitize?

Sanitizing is reducing the unseen germs or pathogens on a surface to safe levels. Germs cannot be completely removed. It is impossible for food service and retail facilities to fully sterilize equipment. The goal of sanitizing is to kill as many germs as possible so people do not get sick.

1. After proper cleaning, sanitize all things that come in contact with food, utensils, cutting boards, and prep tables with approved sanitizers that are listed in the SOP.

2. Clean and sanitize all equipment and in use utensils at a minimum of every 4 hours.

3. You can manually sanitize with hot water that is at least 171°F (77.2°C) or use a chemical sanitizer. Note: Water above 125°F (51.6°C) is a safety hazard (burn). See your manager concerning proper procedures for your food service or retail establishment.

4. When a dishwashing machine is used, the sanitizing process will be based upon the manufacturer's specifications. If you are assigned to dish washing duty, be sure you know and understand how to use the dishwasher, including how to check and test for proper sanitizing heat or chemicals. Do not rely on your dishwasher maintenance company to check your machine monthly. The dishwasher chemicals and/or heat gauges should be checked and verified several times throughout the day. Check your company SOPs.

Your manager will work with you to demonstrate the proper SOP for your food service or retail operation. There are several important points to remember:

- Always use approved sanitizers. Check your company's SOP;
- Always have and use sanitizer test strips;
- Never mix chemicals;
- Use separate cloths for food surfaces (prep table) and non-food surfaces (walls/floors);
- Use a designated sink system like the three-compartment sink to clean and sanitize dishes and utensils;
- Never clean and sanitize dishes in the hand washing sink;
- Mop water can only be emptied into the service or utility sink. Never empty mop water into the toilet or in the three-compartment sink.

How Do You Manually Clean and Sanitize Using a Three-Compartment Sink?

Step 1: Clean and sanitize entire sink before starting.

Step 2: Scrape and rinse dirty dishes.

Step 3: Wash at 110°F (43.3°C) with soapy water.

Step 4: Rinse at 110°F (43.3°C) with clear water.

Step 5: Sanitize using your SOP.

Step 6: Air-dry.

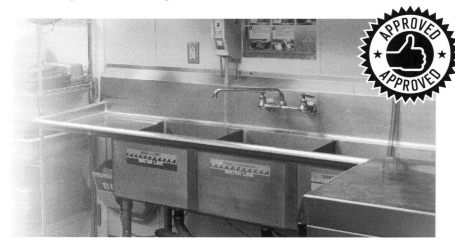

Serving Food and Operating Self-Service Bars

Serving Food

Can you answer YES to any of these questions?

- Do you stack dinner plates and/or coffee cups when serving food/drink to customers?
- Are your fingers on the top or edge of the plate in the food?
- Do you serve, clear tables, answer the phone, and cashier without washing hands?
- Do you recycle rolls, unwrapped butter, uneaten garnishes (pickles) from plates?
- Do you store utensils, towels, or your order pad in your pockets or waistband?
- Do you stack plates against your body and allow body parts (hair) to contaminate the food when carrying food to the table and serving it?

If you answered yes to any of these questions, then the time is now to begin serving food safely. Do not let food safety end in the kitchen! You are an important role in food safety. Servers should never stack dinner plates and cups on top of one another, or on arms, or carry too many in one hand. It is a surefire way to cross contaminate foods… not to mention dropping, spilling, or breaking something.

Today's customer is more educated and will be more aware of servers who bus tables and then touch plates or glasses as they deliver food without washing their hands between each task. This same customer is also aware of the server who answers the phone, writes down an order, prepares the food, and rings the register, and collects the money while wearing the same pair of gloves she wore when going through the same routine for the three previous customers. When you carry a large tray of food to the table, do you rest it on your shoulder where your long hair can dangle into the food on your shoulder? You do not want to be responsible for making customers sick.

You should always carry all utensils by the handle. Make sure all glasses are carried by the side, and all plates from the bottom. Do not store utensils and cloths in your pockets or in the waistband of your clothes.

When you remove glasses or cups from the table for refills, get new glasses. Are you sure you will be returning the correct glass to the correct customer? Do not forget allergens or dietary concerns. The wrong returned refilled glass could land your customer in the hospital. The best practice is to bring the drink to the table and refill glasses right in front of the customers or place old glasses in the dish washing area and use a new glass. Do not pick up the customer's dirty glass. Use a pitcher and fill the glass while it sits on the table. If you touch the customer's dirty glass then pick up another person's glass, you are spreading germs (especially during flu season).

Do not to reuse food like rolls, unwrapped butter, and uneaten pickle garnishes. The safest rule to follow is that any food that leaves your control should **never** be re-served to a customer.

Food Safety for Self-Service Areas

All self-service bars and buffets should be monitored by an employee at all times for both Food Safety and Food Defense purposes. In order to keep food safe at self-service food bars and buffets:

1. Separate raw meats and fish from cooked and RTE food. There are very few raw animal foods that can safely be on self-service bars. They might include shellfish raw bars, Mongolian barbecues and Sushi bars. These raw items, though RTE, should be separated from cooked RTE foods.

2. Monitor customers for unsanitary hygiene practices, such as the following:
   - Tasting items.
   - Handling multiple breads with their bare hands.
   - Putting fingers directly into the food.
   - Reusing plates and utensils; instead, hand out fresh plates to customers.

   Note: Act immediately, if you see a food being contaminated by a customer. Discretely remove the product and alert the PIC.

3. Label all food items.

4. Maintain separate serving utensils in each food type. Serving utensil handles should be long enough to not slide down in the food. The handle should always be up and out of the food.

5. Maintain proper temperatures. Monitor and check frequently.

6. Practice First-In First-Out (FIFO) rotation of products. Always use the oldest product first. When refilling, do not mix the old food and new food together.

7. Do not store an in-use utensil in a container of water with or without sanitizer. In-use utensils (like ice cream scoops and rice spoons) must be kept in cool running water. Other alternatives might exist, but check with your regulator for other approved options for in-use utensil storage.

Star Point 1 Conclusion

Foods may become unsafe accidentally because of cross contamination, poor personal hygiene, improper cleaning and sanitizing, and time–temperature abuse. It's important that you keep the food, yourself, other employees, and your customers safe at all times. Written policies and procedures such as prerequisite programs and standard operating procedures are the building blocks that help every facility keep their food and their customers safe. SOPs are the foundation to which all great HACCP plans are built.

Star Knowledge Exercise:

Food Safety – What Should I Do If

Circle the risk factor(s) that apply to the situation and write in what you would do to correct the problem.

Situation	Risk Factors: a. Cross contamination b. Poor personal hygiene c. Improper cleaning and sanitizing d. Time-temperature abuse	What do you do to correct the situation? Make it a "REAL" solution!
1. A serving utensil falls on the floor.	a. Cross contamination b. Poor personal hygiene c. Improper cleaning and sanitizing d. Time-temperature abuse	
2. An employee wore a dirty uniform to work.	a. Cross contamination b. Poor personal hygiene c. Improper cleaning and sanitizing d. Time-temperature abuse	
3. You are stocking shelves and notice the date on a carton of shell eggs is expired.	a. Cross contamination b. Poor personal hygiene c. Improper cleaning and sanitizing d. Time-temperature abuse	
4. It is 3 p.m. and you find a pan of sausage on the prep table left out since breakfast. Breakfast ended at 11 a.m.	a. Cross contamination b. Poor personal hygiene c. Improper cleaning and sanitizing c. Time-temperature abuse	

Situation	Risk Factors: a. Cross contamination b. Poor personal hygiene c. Improper cleaning and sanitizing d. Time-temperature abuse	What do you do to correct the situation? Make it a "REAL" solution!
5. As a coworker comes out of the bathroom, you see her tying her apron.	a. Cross contamination b. Poor personal hygiene c. Improper cleaning and sanitizing d. Time-temperature abuse	
6. A customer returns a meatball sandwich because it is cold.	a. Cross contamination b. Poor personal hygiene c. Improper cleaning and sanitizing d. Time-temperature abuse	
7. The sanitizer solution is supposed to be 200 ppm (parts per million). You see a new coworker set up the three-compartment sink, but he uses too much sanitizer.	a. Cross contamination b. Poor personal hygiene c. Improper cleaning and sanitizing d. Time-temperature abuse	
8. A customer is allergic to fish. The server tells the cook that her customer has a fish allergy. The customer ordered a hamburger but there is only one spatula on the production line that is used for everything.	a. Cross contamination b. Poor personal hygiene c. Improper cleaning and sanitizing d. Time-temperature abuse	
9. Right before closing you are cleaning the walls in the food service area. A customer rushes in and places an order.	a. Cross contamination b. Poor personal hygiene c. Improper cleaning and sanitizing d. Time-temperature abuse	
10. A coworker is angry with a disgruntled customer and spits on the customer's plate.	a. Cross contamination b. Poor personal hygiene c. Improper cleaning and sanitizing d. Time-temperature abuse	

Star Point 1 Check for Understanding

(Circle one.)

1. HACCP stands for _____ .
   a. Hazard Analysis, Cooking and Cooling Procedures
   b. Hazard Analysis Critical Control Point
   c. Help Analyze Chicken Cooking Points
   d. Hazard Analysis and Critical Control Point

2. Standard Operating Procedures (SOP) are _____ .
   a. acceptable practices and procedures for your operation
   b. written documents regarding your employment
   c. 7 steps in the food flow process
   d. all of the above

3. Which of the following is NOT a Big 6 Pathogen?
   a. E. Coli
   b. Shigella
   c. Norovirus
   d. Hepatitis B

4. The Temperature Danger Zone (TDZ) is _____ .
   a. 41°F – 135°F (5°C – 57.2°C)
   b. 70°F – 140°F (21.1°C – 60°C)
   c. 41°F – 165°F (5°C – 73.8°C)
   d. 0°F – 212°F (-17.7°C – 100°C)

5. Prerequisite programs _____ .
   a. require that all food employees take a national food safety exam
   b. require that all food employees have a physical exam before beginning work in a food facility
   c. define acceptable practices and procedures for the entire food service or retail establishment and its employees
   d. both a and c

HACCP Star Point 2:
Apply Food Defense

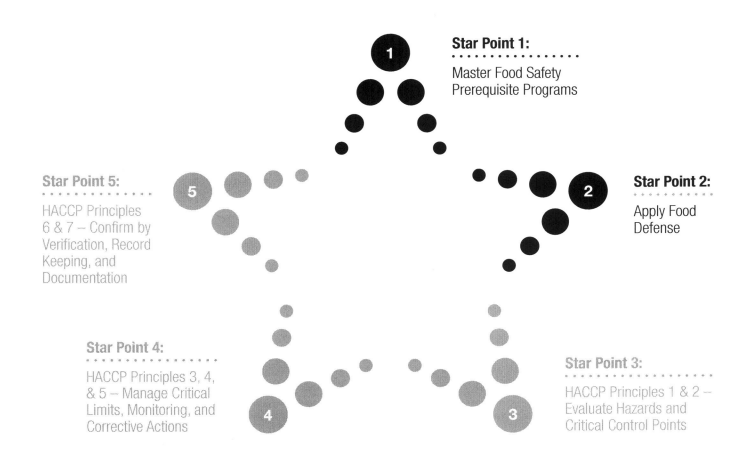

Star Point 1:

Master Food Safety
Prerequisite Programs

Star Point 2:

Apply Food
Defense

Star Point 3:

HACCP Principles 1 & 2 –
Evaluate Hazards and
Critical Control Points

Star Point 4:

HACCP Principles 3, 4,
& 5 – Manage Critical
Limits, Monitoring, and
Corrective Actions

Star Point 5:

HACCP Principles
6 & 7 – Confirm by
Verification, Record
Keeping, and
Documentation

Star Point 2 Myth or Fact (Check one.)

1. Food defense and food safety mean the same thing.
____**Myth** ____**Fact**

2. Leaving your back door open on a hot day could threaten food defense.
____**Myth** ____**Fact**

3. Always ask for identification when receiving deliveries.
____**Myth** ____**Fact**

4. Always report any potential threat to management immediately.
____**Myth** ____**Fact**

5. You do not need to worry about the security of the outside of your building.
____**Myth** ____**Fact**

Star Point 2 Goals

You will learn to:

- Differentiate between food defense, food safety, and food security;
- Explain why food defense is so important;
- Apply food defense SOPs to handle different situations; and
- Discuss your role in food defense as a responsible employee.

In Star Point 2, we will discuss the basics of food defense. We must understand how food can become contaminated so that we can create food defense standard operating procedures to prevent problems from occurring. This is part of an effective HACCP plan. Food defense prerequisite programs can then be incorporated into a HACCP plan. Ask your manager if there is a food defense plan in your operation.

Introduction to Food Defense

We must be concerned with food defense, food safety, and food security. Unfortunately, acts of food terrorism both foreign and domestic have already been documented and have caused injury and death. As a responsible employee, you should educate yourself about the safety issues in your operation, the food industry, and the entire country. We must make every effort to identify and stop any potential deliberate food contamination. As an employee in the food service or retail industry, it is your responsibility to take action! Each country, the United Nations, and the World Health Organization define Food Safety, Food Security, and Food Defense differently. However, definitions of these three challenges to the supply of safe food are presented below;

Food Defense

Food Defense is the prevention of the **deliberate contamination** of food. Note that the action of the person contaminating the food is deliberate and not accidental. These individuals and their actions are designed to cause harm to people.

Food Safety

Food Safety is the prevention of the **accidental contamination** of food. This accidental and unintentional contamination occurs from chemical, biological, or physical hazards.

Food Security

Food Security is the ability to **ensure a 2-year food supply** for a particular country. Though very important, this topic is not covered in this book.

No matter how these items are defined, by any given organization, together they each are very important to providing the safest supply of food to the public.

Understanding Food Defense and Employee Responsibilities

Food defense is very simple to practice; be aware, and pay attention to your surroundings, fellow employees, customers, vendors, and your facility. No one knows a work environment better than the current employees who work there. Does something seem different? Is something out of place? Do not let something out of sorts go unreported. Do not get complaisant (or lazy) about your work environment and think… 'That would never happen in THIS food service or retail establishment'. Be prepared! Though it may not happen often, food tampering, food hoaxes, and deliberate food contamination can and has happened. Do not be overly distrustful or paranoid. The best defense is to simply be alert and aware of your environment…with a few daily precautions always in place. Food Defense SOPs will help employees know what to do to protect their workplace and customers. This will also define what to do if you suspect or become aware of a food defense issue.

Your responsibility as an employee is to prepare, serve, and sell safe food. Understanding Food Defense will protect you, your family, your business, and the food service or retail industry. The FDA recommends you take Food Defense steps to ensure the safety of customers, coworkers, and country. Standard operating procedures will assure that, as an employee, you understand your responsibility and what an important role you play in Food Defense every day. The recommendations include the following Awareness SOPs.

Employee Awareness SOP

- **Be a responsible employee.** Communicate any potential food defense issues to your manager.
- **Be aware** of your surroundings and pay attention to employees who are acting unusual, different from their normal behavior.
- Limit the amount of personal items brought into your work establishment.
- Be aware of who is working at a given time and where (in what area) they are supposed to be working.
- If you are assigned to the salad bar, self-service food, or displays, constantly monitor them. Let customers know there is employee presence in that area. Salad bars and open food displays are easy targets for someone wanting to do harm.
- Make sure labeled chemicals are in a designated storage area away from food and not easily accessible.
- Make sure you and your coworkers are following company guidelines. If you have any questions or believe company guidelines are not being followed, please ask your manager to assist you.
- Take all threats seriously, even if it is a fellow coworker or customer blowing off steam. Report it!
- If the back door is supposed to be locked and secure, make sure it is!
- Look at food products every day for irregularities. If you use a food product and it is supposed to be green but today it is blue, stop using the product and notify your manager immediately.
- If you know an employee is no longer with your company and this person enters an "Employee Only" area, notify your manager immediately.
- Strangers and friends of employees should never be in the food prep area.
- Cooperate during all investigations.
- Do not talk to the media; refer all questions to your corporate office or an official spokesperson.
- If you are aware of a hoax or threat, notify your manager immediately.

Customer Awareness SOP

- Be aware of any unattended bags or briefcases that customers bring into your operation.
- Be aware of any unusual behavior of customers. Some examples of unusual behaviors are uneasiness, pacing around, and attempts to enter areas that are not for customers.
- Monitor salad bars and self-service food areas or open food displays for any unusual customer activity.
- If a customer walks into an "Employee Only" area of your operation, ask the customer politely if he/she needs help, then notify a member of management.

Vendor Awareness SOP

Vendors and service personal are commonplace in food service and retail establishments. They tend to come and go. Employees and managers pay little attention to what they are doing while in the establishment. We assume they know what they are there for and allow then to go about their business. Unfortunately, this can also be an easy entrance for someone wanting to do harm.

Always ask for identification of any vendor or service person that enters restricted areas of your establishment. If you do not recognize the regular delivery person, ask for ID.

- When items are being delivered, stay with the delivery person.
- Monitor all products received and look for any signs of tampering. Do not accept questionable deliveries.
- Never accept items that are not listed on your invoice. If the vendor attempts to give you additional items not listed, notify your manager.
- If a service person arrives, do they have an approved work order? Where are they scheduled to do work in the facility? If you are unsure, verify with your manager.
- Do not allow vendors or service persons to roam freely throughout your operation.
- Also, though not a vendor or service person, you should always ask for identification from your inspector or any person claiming to be a government or regulatory employee.

Facility Awareness SOP

- Report and document all equipment, maintenance, and security issues to your manager.
- Be aware of the inside of your facility including unusually open doors and windows.
- Be observant with the outside of the facility, including the dumpster and outside storage areas.
- Always report anything out of the ordinary.

Dealing with Hoaxes

Equally damaging are false accusations or fraudulent reports of deliberate contamination of food. As a responsible employee, you must notify your manager if you suspect a false alarm has occurred.

An example of a hoax: A person posted on the internet that she found a horrifying object in her food that was sold by Company XYZ. After investigation, the statements were confirmed to be not true. This hoax is damaging to the employees, the company, the brand, and the food industry. Stories like this negatively affect everyone!

Awareness

Read the story below and answer the questions about the food defense concerns in this situation.

Dan is the manager of an establishment in a large city, and he is scheduled to work the morning shift. As soon as Dan's shift begins, two employees call in sick. One employee was scheduled to work the lunch shift, and the other was scheduled to unload the truck. Dan calls all of the other employees to see if they can work, but no one can come in and help.

Dan tells Bob, the morning prep person, about the situation. The two of them will be the only employees working through lunch. Bob will be responsible for unloading the truck while Dan will run the register and take care of the customer's food.

When the truck arrives, both Dan and Bob are doing everything they can to keep up with the busy lunch rush. Neither of them has time to help unload the truck, so the vendor unloads the truck alone and leaves the food on the loading dock. Two hours later, Dan and Bob work together to bring the food into the establishment.

Which food defense related "Awareness SOP" was not being followed? (Check all that apply.)

❏ Employee Awareness SOP   ❏ Vendor Awareness SOP
❏ Customer Awareness SOP   ❏ Facility Awareness SOP

Can you think of a way to run a safer operation?_____

_____

_____

_____

Star Point 2 Conclusion

- Food Defense is not a guessing game; it is all about the facts! If you suspect or observe something out of the ordinary report it as soon as possible: who, what, where, and when!
- Always report any potential threat to management immediately!
- Doing nothing at all is still taking an action and potentially dangerous!

Star Knowledge Exercise:

Food Defense – What Should I Do If

What can you do to provide Food Defense for your customers, your coworkers, your country, and the business you represent?

Consider the following…Should you get involved if you suspect something is not quite right with your food service or retail operation on a given day? Yes or No?

Think about the following examples. Is the scenario a food defense concern? What would you do?

Situation	Is this a concern? Yes or no?	What do you do?	
1. You see a coworker behaving in a suspicious manner. You know the coworker has contaminated food, but you do not know if it was done accidentally or deliberately.	Yes No		
2. A customer wanders into an "Employee-Only" area.	Yes No		
3. A fellow coworker is upset and starts talking about ways he is going to harm the manager and the company. He only seems to be blowing off steam.	Yes No		
4. A customer brings a large duffel bag into your operation.	Yes No		

Situation	Is this a concern? Yes or no?	What do you do?
5. An ex-coworker, loved by everyone, wanders into the "Employee-Only" area to say hello to everyone.	Yes No	
6. A vendor walks through the back door with a delivery.	Yes No	
7. A vendor is making a delivery. The manager ordered 7 containers of a certain food item, but the vendor wants to give you an extra container.	Yes No	
8. You walk by the food bar and see a spray bottle of glass cleaner sitting on it.	Yes No	
9. An incident happened in your operation causing a customer to become seriously ill. As you walk to your vehicle, a news reporter approaches you.	Yes No	
10. You are in the process of preparing food for the day and you pull a can off the shelf. There is a small hole in the top of the can.	Yes No	

Resources: www.gao.gov • www.fda.gov • www.dhs.gov • www.fsis.usda.gov • www.usda.gov • www.epa.gov

Star Point 2 Check For Understanding
(Circle one.)

1. Which scenarios could effect the safety of the food in your facility?
   a. leaving the back door open
   b. allowing a service person to roam freely in the facility
   c. not reporting suspicious activity
   d. all of the above

2. Food defense is_____ .
   a. preventing accidental contamination of food
   b. preventing intentional contamination to food
   c. having a 2 year supply of food
   d. having a strong military

3. Food security is_____ .
   a. preventing accidental contamination of food
   b. preventing intentional contamination to food
   c. having a 2 year supply of food
   d. having a strong military

4. When a vendor arrives, you should always _____ .
   a. tell him to put the supplies in the storage area
   b. check his identification
   c. stay with him while he is in the facility
   d. both b and c

5. Food Defense SOPs do not include_____ .
   a. facility awareness
   b. employee health awareness
   c. vendor awareness
   d. customer awareness

HACCP Star Point 3:
HACCP Principles 1 & 2 – Evaluate Hazards
and Critical Control Points

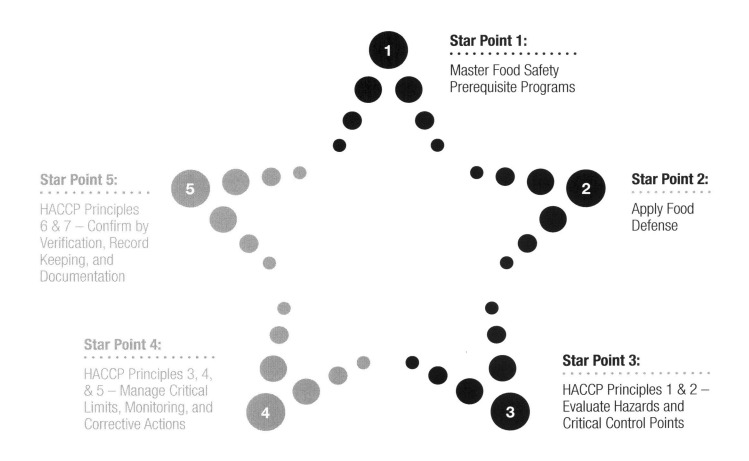

Star Point 1:
Master Food Safety
Prerequisite Programs

Star Point 2:
Apply Food
Defense

Star Point 3:
HACCP Principles 1 & 2 –
Evaluate Hazards and
Critical Control Points

Star Point 5:
HACCP Principles
6 & 7 – Confirm by
Verification, Record
Keeping, and
Documentation

Star Point 4:
HACCP Principles 3, 4,
& 5 – Manage Critical
Limits, Monitoring, and
Corrective Actions

Star Point 3 Myth or Fact (Check one.)

1. A HACCP plan must identify potential hazards in the flow of food.
　　___**Myth** ___**Fact**

2. HACCP was developed for the U.S. space program.
　　___**Myth** ___**Fact**

3. Hazard analysis looks for potential hazards that will occur in a food service or retail establishment.
　　___**Myth** ___**Fact**

4. Every recipe or food in the operation must have a specific HACCP Plan.
　　___**Myth** ___**Fact**

5. Some points in the flow of food are more critical than others, they are called Critical Control Points (CCP).
　　___**Myth** ___**Fact**

Star Point 3 Goals

You will learn to:

- Define HACCP;
- Summarize why HACCP is important;
- Describe the flow of food;
- Describe the HACCP philosophy and define your role;
- Practice conducting a hazard analysis (HACCP Principle 1); and
- Determine critical control points (HACCP Principle 2).

In Star Point 3, we will learn two of the seven principles of a HACCP Plan. Earlier, we established that prerequisite programs and SOPs for food safety and food defense are the foundation for an effective HACCP plan. In addition, your manager/ director should have reviewed program basics (SOPs) such as facility design, equipment, pest control, chemical control, cleaning and sanitizing procedures, responsible employee practices, food specifications, and food temperature control with you.

HACCP Introduction

What is HACCP?

HACCP ("has-sip") is an abbreviation for Hazard Analysis and Critical Control Point. It is a food safety system that prevents disasters, such as foodborne illness outbreaks, from occurring. It is a system that follows the flow of food from when and how it is purchased to delivery to the consumer. In this book, we are focusing on food service and retail establishments implementing HACCP. How do you control the risk of foodborne illness in these settings?

As you now know, foodborne illness occurs when you eat food and something in it makes you sick. As you learned in Star Point 1, the CDC lists the five most common **risk factors** that create foodborne illness:

    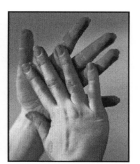

| **Food From Unsafe Sources** | **Inadequate Cooking** | **Improper Holding Temperatures** | **Contaminated Equipment** | **Poor Personal Hygiene** |

Remember, an outbreak occurs when two or more people eat the same food and get the same illness. HACCP helps prevent foodborne illness outbreaks because HACCP is a **proactive approach** to control risk factors at every step in the flow of food. Simply stated, the **HACCP goal is to prevent, eliminate, and reduce food safety problems**.

HACCP is a written food safety system to enable you to serve safe food. The HACCP food safety system has 7 principles. You will learn about all 7 principles in the next three Star Point sections.

For many operations, like food manufacturers or a public school system, having a HACCP plan in place is mandated by the government. Though most states do not mandate Retail HACCP, it is just as important to this industry as it is to other food industries.

Although you may not be involved in the development of the HACCP plan, you do need to understand how it was developed in order to carry out your part of the plan effectively. Every person in the food service or retail establishment is critical to the safe preparation and service of food. No matter what your job description and duties are, you will benefit from understanding and knowing the HACCP system. Someday, who knows, you may be asked to be a member of a HACCP Team—A person who helps develops your company's HACCP plan.

Why is HACCP Important?

To understand why HACCP is important, you need to first familiarize yourself with the history of the HACCP program. HACCP was originally designed in the early 1960s by National Aeronautics and Space Administration (NASA) and the Pillsbury Company for the U.S. space program. Yes, the HACCP program was actually developed by rocket scientists! The reason why they developed the program was to prevent the astronauts from getting sick in space.

All food has microorganisms, which is why NASA needed a food safety system that would prevent, eliminate, and reduce the number of microorganisms to safe levels. They needed to prevent a foodborne illness from occurring in space. Can you imagine an astronaut in space who is vomiting and has diarrhea?

After NASA incorporated HACCP plans, the military, manufacturers, schools, and, in some jurisdictions, retailers have seen how effective HACCP is at preventing foodborne illness. Ask your manager if your operation is required by law to have a HACCP plan or do they have a HACCP plan on a voluntary basis?

Now that we know the history of HACCP and why it became necessary to incorporate a HACCP plan, let's take a look at the HACCP philosophy.

The HACCP Philosphy

HACCP is now internationally accepted.

HACCP is not a process conducted by an individual; it involves the **entire team**. This is why you are a part of this training session. Your manager/director is counting on you to do your part in preventing foodborne illness in your food service or retail operation and in your part of the world.

The **HACCP philosophy** simply states that biological, chemical, or physical hazards, at certain points in the flow of food, can be:

- **Prevented;**
- **Eliminated;** or
- **Reduced to safe levels.**

Not too long ago, food was either picked or bought personally at the local store or from the community. Today, our food supply is globalized with food transported around the world more than ever before. The eating habits of people around the world have also changed. With busy lives, people eat out more often, consume more ready-to-eat foods, enjoy more etåic dishes, and explore different foods. Customers want fresh produce in the middle of winter. Tomatoes from South America, grapes from Europe, fruits from Southeast Asia all come to the United States and are sold in supermarkets. Here is the problem; the more food products are touched by people or machines, the greater the opportunity for contamination, or, even worse, the greater the opportunity to spread a foodborne illness. This is why we need HACCP!

To begin development of a HACCP plan, the HACCP team must first conduct a hazard analysis. If this is your responsibility as a member of the HACCP team, then you will

1. Identify the hazards associated with preparing food **(Hazard Analysis)**.

2. After identifying these hazards, you will divide the food service or retail establishment's menu based on how each food is prepared.

3. As each grouping of food is prepared, you must determine what steps you need to take in order to prepare those foods safely. These are called critical control points.

Let's get started with Principle 1.

HACCP Principle 1: Conduct a Hazard Analysis

A **hazard analysis** is the first HACCP principle in evaluating foods in your food service or retail operation. This is the first step to identify any TCS food used in your establishment. **The analysis identifies potential hazards that are reasonably likely to occur in your operation.** It is important to separate food safety from food quality. A hazard analysis focuses on food safety, **not** food quality. Consider the following: A certain food might be dried out by one or more reheating steps. It may have lost some of its appeal to a customer, but it is still safe to eat. This is diminished food quality. If the food were reheated improperly, then there would be a food safety concern. Food Safety ≠ Food Quality.

The key to a successful HACCP program is to conduct a thorough hazard analysis. If the hazards are not correctly identified, the risks to your program increase significantly, and the program will not be effective.

There are **4 primary steps in conducting a hazard analysis**:

1. Identify TCS foods. Remember, not all foods are potentially hazardous. See Star Point 1 if you need to review.

2. Understand the flow of food to determine where hazards may be controlled.

3. Divide menu items into 3 categories by how the food is prepared.

4. Hazard analysis questions:
   • What is the likelihood of a hazard to occur here?
   • What is the risk if the hazard does occur?
   • Is there a way for this hazard to be controlled or eliminated?

Let's explore these steps in detail.

Identify Time/Temperature Control for Safety of Food

To analyze the food in your establishment, the first thing to do is to identify all TCS food. All TCS foods must be addressed in a HACCP plan. Remember, not all foods are potentially hazardous.

Apply what you learned in Star Point 1. Using this sample menu, can you identify any TCS foods?

TCS Foods

Place a check mark in the box next to any item that is TCS.

Sample Menu

Starters:

❑ Vegetable Tray with from scratch buttermilk ranch dip

❑ Chicken Noodle Soup

❑ Salsa and Chips

Entrées:

❑ Salmon Stuffed with Crabmeat

❑ Popcorn Shrimp

❑ Hamburger

❑ Tuna Salad

Side Dishes:

❑ Garden Salad with from scratch bleu cheese dressing

❑ Cole Slaw

❑ Grilled Vegetables

❑ Pickled Beets

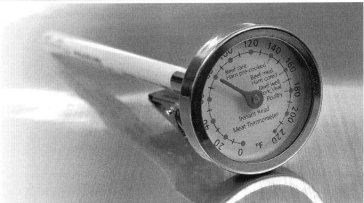

Flow of Food

Purchase
▼
Receive
▼
Store
▼
Prepare
▼
Cook
▼
Hold
▼
Cool
▼
Reheat
▼
Serve

In order to determine where hazards may be controlled, you need to understand the flow of food. All the food we eat goes through what we call a **flow of food**. All flows of food start with the purchasing of food from approved sources. The food is then received, stored, prepared, cooked, held, cooled, reheated, and served.

The flow of food can be described by looking at how you make a pot of home-made soup. First, you **purchase** the ingredients from a clean, safe grocery store. You take the food you purchased and **receive** the food into your home; then you need to store the food properly either in dry storage (your cabinets or pantry), or in your refrigerator and freezer. Once the food is **stored** properly, you then **prepare** the food (slicing vegetables, portioning meats, etc.). After preparation, the product is cooked. To **cook** your homemade soup properly, it must reach a minimum temperature of 165°F (73.9°C) for < 1 second. Once the soup has reached 165°F (73.9°C), then you can **hold** the soup. The correct hot holding temperature for your delicious homemade soup is 135°F (57.2°C) or above. The next step in the flow of food is to **cool** the unused soup for storage in your refrigerator. The proper way to cool soup is to bring it to 41°F (5°C) as quickly as possible (follow the cooling process you learned in Star Point 1). The next day, you see the soup in your refrigerator and decide to **reheat** it. The soup must be reheated to 165°F (73.9°C) for 15 seconds within 2 hours before it is safe. The final step is to **serve** the soup and enjoy.

Chicken Noodle Soup

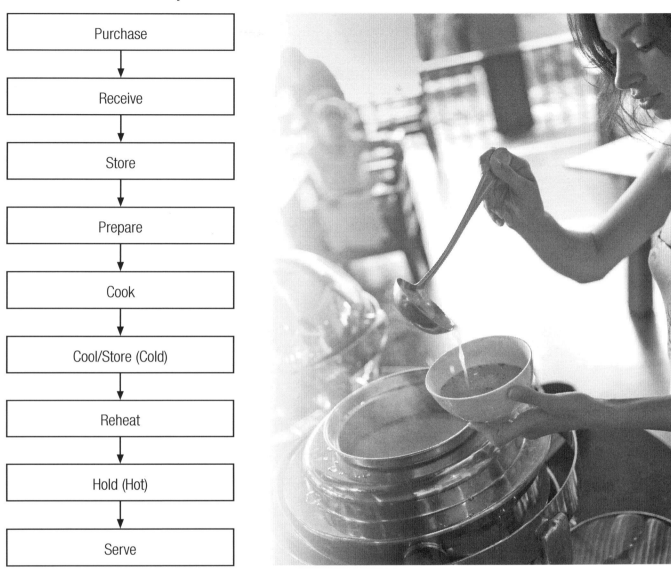

Purchase

↓

Receive

↓

Store

↓

Prepare

↓

Cook

↓

Cool/Store (Cold)

↓

Reheat

↓

Hold (Hot)

↓

Serve

Remember, the flow of food is **purchase, receive, store, prepare, cook, hold, cool, reheat, and serve**. HACCP helps you to ensure that at every step in the flow of food, the food stays safe. In our example, no one got sick by eating the home-made soup because the well trained team member followed the food safety SOPs in the flow of food. It is necessary for all food establishments to set the same goal—to serve safe food.

Pop Quiz:

Flow of Food

In this activity identify the steps in the flow of food for tuna salad and a hamburger. Determine the steps and write them in the correct order in the boxes. Different establishments with different preparation procedures or ingredients could have the same food item, but use different steps in the flow of food.

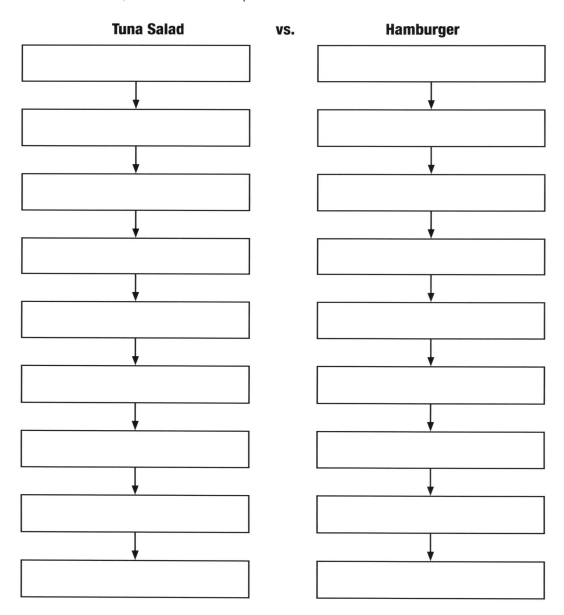

Tuna Salad   vs.   Hamburger

* Notice some recipes may have more steps than others. For example: Tuna Salad can be a Simple/No-Cook recipe and also can be a Complex recipe if a hard-boiled egg is added to the salad.

Divide the Menu into Categories

Once the flow of food is determined for your menu items, you should then divide your menu items into 1 of 3 categories by how the item is prepared. You do not need to develop a HACCP Plan for every food item. Many items are similar in how they are prepared. There are three ways to divide the menu: Simple/No-Cook, Same-Day, and Complex.

A **Simple/No-Cook** recipe means exactly that: there is **no cooking** involved. For example, when tuna salad is prepared, a can or bag of tuna is opened, drained of the juice, placed in a bowl, mayonnaise, and seasonings are added, it is mixed well, chilled, and served.

Other foods your HACCP plan might identify as Simple/No-Cook recipes include:

- Cheese platter
- Cole slaw
- Vegetable tray

A **Same-Day** recipe means a food product is prepared for same-day service or has some same-day cooking involved. If a **food moves through the temperature danger zone one time**, it is considered a same-day recipe. For example, a hamburger requires that you take the frozen hamburger patty from the freezer, place the hamburger on the grill, cook the hamburger to 155°F (68.3°C) for 15 seconds, place the cooked hamburger on a bun, and serve. Other foods your HACCP plan might identify as Same-Day recipes include:

- Chicken sandwich
- Popcorn shrimp
- Grilled vegetables

A **Complex** recipe calls for a food to be prepared, cooled, stored, and then reheated. If a **food moves through the temperature danger zone two or more times**, it is considered a Complex recipe. The homemade soup described earlier is an example of a Complex recipe.

When using a Complex recipe you must:

1. Determine the potential for microorganisms to
   a. Survive a heat process (cooking or reheating)
   b. Multiply at room temperature and during hot and cold holding.

2. Find potential sources and specific points of contamination within the recipe.

Other foods your HACCP plan might identify as Complex recipes include:

- Soup
- Lasagna
- Salmon stuffed with crabmeat

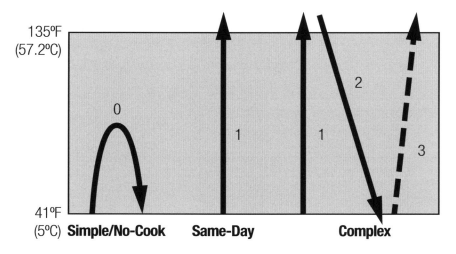

Complete Trips Through the Danger Zone

135ºF
(57.2ºC)

0

1

2

1

3

41ºF
(5ºC) **Simple/No-Cook**   **Same-Day**   **Complex**

Depicted above is the FDA Danger Zone diagram that summarized the three food preparation processes in terms of number of times food passes through the temperature danger zone.

Hazard Analysis Questions

Answer these questions as part of the hazard analysis.

What is the likelihood of a hazard occurring?

As we discussed in Star Point 1, most hazards are **biological** (bacteria, viruses, and parasites). Other hazards might be **chemical** (cleaning products, sanitizers, and pesticides) or **physical** (metal shavings, foreign objects, and hair). In the tuna salad, hamburger, and chicken noodle soup, what is the likelihood for this to occur? What are the chances these hazards could contaminate the food?

What is the risk if the hazard does occur?

If there is a **high risk** of contamination, does it lead to an unacceptable health risk? **An unacceptable health risk can lead to injury, illness, or death.** Or is the risk of contamination low, meaning an acceptable health risk? Acceptable risks are those that present little or no chance of injury, illness, or death. Experts use scientific data to determine if the risk is high or low for each hazard that is analyzed. HACCP teams usually have an expert on the team to help evaluate hazards and their risks.

Is there a way to control or eliminate this hazard?

The reason why biological, chemical, and physical hazards must be identified and rated for risk is to determine whether a **preventive measure** exists or is needed to control the hazard.

Control measures are actions that can be used to prevent a hazard from occurring. They can eliminate or reduce the hazard to acceptable levels. You will find that some control measures are crucial and other hazards less so.

In Star Point 1 we discussed various food safety procedures in the Food Code. Many of these items such as cooking, cooling, time and temperature control, employee health and hygiene are all control measures that will be applied to the HACCP plan we develop as we continue in the book. We do not live in a sterile or perfect world. But all hazards can be controlled.

For example; in cooking chicken soup, the **biological hazard** is *Salmonella* (highly contagious) and *Campylobacter*, two bacteria highly associated with poultry. The facilities SOPs will describe that a **preventive measure** is to cook the chicken soup to 165°F (73.9°C) < 1 second to kill the *Salmonella* and *Campylobacter* on the chicken. By following this SOP (cook, a control measure) the hazard is prevented, eliminated, or reduced to safe levels.

Control measures to prevent, eliminate, and reduce hazards will always include employee hygiene and prevention of cross contamination. Other more specific control measures, depending on the food and flow of the food, may include minimum cook temperatures, cooling times, reheating times and temperature, refrigeration of RTE foods, and time/temperature control of TCS foods.

Here are a few common foods, an associated hazard and a few examples of control measures:

Product	Hazard	Control Measure
Ground Beef	E. Coli	Cooking
Lunchmeat	Listeria	Good sanitation; Employee health and hygiene; Cold Holding
RTE Salad/ Cut Leafy Greens	Hepatitis A	Approved source; Good sanitation; good employee health and hygiene
Cooked Rice	Bacillus	Cooking; Hot Holding; Cooling according to parameters

As you can see, this is why a Hazard Analysis is so important in a HACCP plan. Once you have conducted the hazard analysis (identified TCS foods, determined food flow, divided foods into categories and analyzed hazards and control measures), you are ready to move to HACCP principle 2 and identify the critical control points.

HACCP Principle 2: Determine Critical Control Points

HACCP Principle 2 is to determine critical control points by first identifying all the control points in the flow of food. This helps you to identify which point(s) are more critical than others. If critical control points are not identified and controlled the likelihood of a foodborne illness increases. Before determining control points and critical control points, you need a clear understanding of what they are.

1. **Control Point (CP)**—This is **any point**, in a step, or procedure at which biological, physical, or chemical factors can be controlled. If loss of control occurs at this point and there is only a **minor chance** of contamination and there is **not an unacceptable health risk**, then the control point is not critical.

2. **Critical Control Point (CCP)**—This is **an essential step** in the product handling process where a food safety hazard can be prevented, eliminated, or reduced to acceptable levels. A critical control point is **one of the last chances you have to be sure the food will be safe when you serve it**. It is the "critical" step that prevents or slows microbial growth, such as proper cooking, cooling, or hot/cold holding. Every operation is different, so critical control points will vary from one operation to another. While not every step in the flow of food will be a CCP, there will be a CCP in at least one or more steps whenever a time/temperature control for safety of food is in the recipe. An operation must control the hazards at this point to avoid an unacceptable health risk. That is why it is critical.

Critical Control Point (CCP) Guidelines

To identify critical control points, ask the following important questions. If you answer **"yes"** to all these points at any stage in the preparation process, you have identified a critical control point.

- Can the food you are preparing become contaminated? (Ask yourself…by what?)
- Can contaminants multiply?
- Can contaminants survive?
- Can you take corrective action(s) to prevent this hazard?
- Is this the last chance you have to prevent, eliminate, or reduce hazards before you serve the food to a customer?

In order to identify the critical control points of a food item, we must first identify the control points, and then determine the most important step(s) that will prevent, eliminate, or reduce the harmful microorganisms to a safe level.

Food Flow Chart Example—Simple/No-Cook Recipe

Tuna Salad

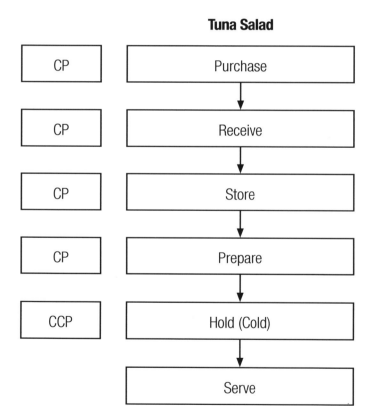

CP	Purchase
CP	Receive
CP	Store
CP	Prepare
CCP	Hold (Cold)
	Serve

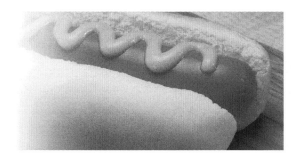

Star Knowledge Exercise:
Identifying CPs & CCPs

Same-Day Recipe—Hamburger

Decide if each step is a control point (CP) or a critical control point (CCP) by circling the correct answer.

(Circle one.)   **Hamburger**

CP CCP	Purchase
CP CCP	Receive
CP CCP	Store
CP CCP	Prepare
CP CCP	Cook
CP CCP	Hold (Hot)
	Serve

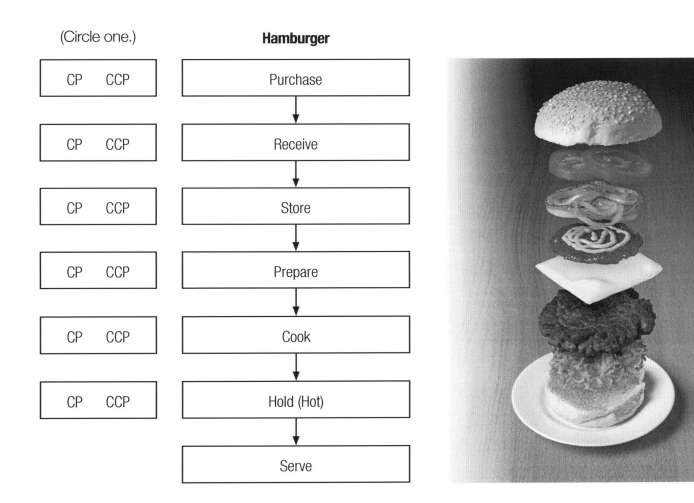

Complex Recipe—Chicken Noodle Soup

Decide if each step is a control point (CP) or a critical control point (CCP) by circling the correct answer.

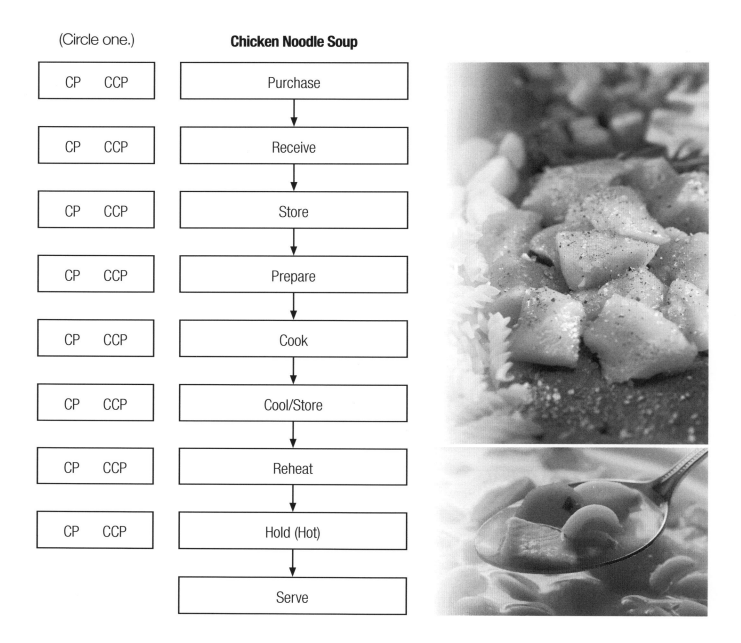

(Circle one.)	Chicken Noodle Soup
CP CCP	Purchase
CP CCP	Receive
CP CCP	Store
CP CCP	Prepare
CP CCP	Cook
CP CCP	Cool/Store
CP CCP	Reheat
CP CCP	Hold (Hot)
	Serve

Star Point 3 Conclusion

In Star Point 3, we discussed how to begin setting up a HACCP plan and how to identify the hazards associated with preparing food. After learning how to identify these hazards, we learned to divide a menu into simple, same-day, and complex recipes. This laid the foundation for the flow of food, control points, and critical control points that we identified in the last exercise.

Star Point 3 Check for Understanding

(Circle one.)

1. Any step in the food flow process where a hazard can be controlled is called a _____ .
   a. Critical Control Point (CCP)
   b. Hazard Analysis and Critical Control Point (HACCP)
   c. Control Point (CP)
   d. Temperature Danger Zone (TDZ)

2. Your menu can be divided into what three basic categories?
   a. Cooked, RTE, and Frozen
   b. Simple/No-Cook, Same-Day, and Complex
   c. Same-Day, Complex, and Multi-Layered

3. HACCP focuses on _____ .
   a. food quality
   b. food safety
   c. both a and b
   d. neither a nor b

4. A Critical Control Point is _____ .
   a. a point where you check invoices
   b. one of the last steps where you can prevent, eliminate, or reduce a food safety hazard
   c. the point where food is thawed
   d. the point where food is served

5. Which of the following is NOT a TCS food?
   a. Foil-Wrapped Baked Potato
   b. Chocolate Chip Cookie
   c. Tossed Salad with Grape Tomatoes
   d. Cut Watermelon

You are making good progress!

HACCP Star Point 4:
HACCP Principles 3, 4, & 5 – Manage Critical Limits, Monitoring, and Corrective Actions

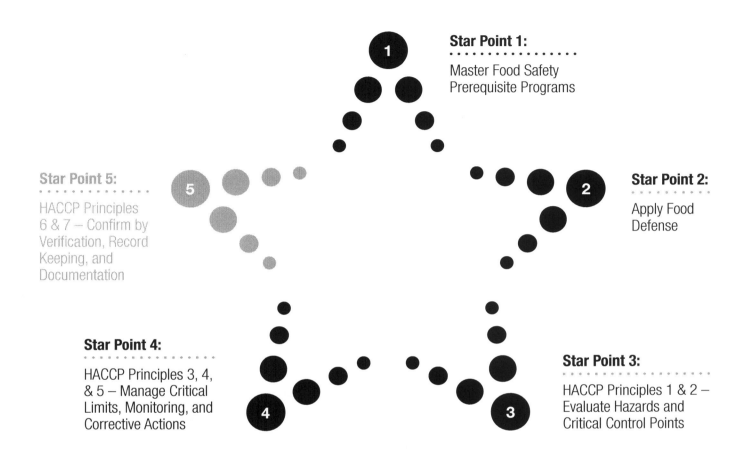

Star Point 1:
Master Food Safety
Prerequisite Programs

Star Point 2:
Apply Food
Defense

Star Point 3:
HACCP Principles 1 & 2 –
Evaluate Hazards and
Critical Control Points

Star Point 4:
HACCP Principles 3, 4,
& 5 – Manage Critical
Limits, Monitoring, and
Corrective Actions

Star Point 5:
HACCP Principles
6 & 7 – Confirm by
Verification, Record
Keeping, and
Documentation

Star Point 4 Myth or Fact (Check one.)

1. Critical Limits are prescribed parameters for CCPs.
___**Myth** ___**Fact**

2. Monitoring is only something that you need to do monthly.
___**Myth** ___**Fact**

3. Corrective Actions are acts taken by employees when critical limits are not met.
___**Myth** ___**Fact**

4. Critical Limits are not based on scientific research and proven fact.
___**Myth** ___**Fact**

5. Monitoring is the act of observing and making measurements.
___**Myth** ___**Fact**

Star Point 4 Goals

You will learn to:

- Establish critical limits (HACCP Principle 3);
- Define monitoring procedures (HACCP Principle 4); and
- Determine corrective actions (HACCP Principle 5).

In Star Point 4, we will learn control measures and critical limits, such as minimum and maximum times and temperatures, for the critical control points covered in the previous chapter. **This is the most important Star Point because this is where you "work the plan" through monitoring times and temperatures and taking the appropriate corrective actions to keep food safe.**

HACCP Principle 3: Establish Critical Limits

Now that we have completed the hazard analysis and identified control points and critical control points, our next step is to look at critical limits. A **critical limit** is based on a proven fact from experience or research data and is typically addressed in food regulations. It is the **scientific measurement** that must be met for each critical control point. A critical limit is like a traffic speed limit on a major highway. There is always a minimum or maximum speed. If you do not drive the minimum speed or if you exceed the maximum speed both are dangerous and you could get stopped and receive a ticket. Critical limits are the same in food preparation; if you do not cook the food to a specific minimum temperature and maximum time, people may be stopped with a foodborne illness.

Not only are critical limits scientific and measurable, they need to be specific and must clearly indicate what needs to be done. For example, if a recipe for baked chicken says "cook until done" or "cook until juices run clear," is the product really safe to eat? The answer is, using those instructions we just do not know. The correct critical limit should say "cook to an internal temperature of 165°F (73.9°C) for < 1 seconds." Why? Scientific data and reference resources from the Food Code provides us with documentation that pathogens will be reduced or eliminated to a safe level if the chicken is cooked to the designated temperature and time which will make it safe to eat.

Every control measure noted for a CCP has at least one measurable critical limit. What can be measured? Definitely time and temperature in various steps of the flow of food! For instance, each TCS food has a minimum internal cooking temperature that must be reached and held for a specific amount of time at that temperature to ensure that it is safe and does not make anyone sick. The act of cooling a TCS food has parameters that determine the length of time food can remain in the temperature danger zone. Think back to Star Point 1 where we discussed various food safety SOPs, you will recall all of the measurable factors that when properly followed keep people from getting ill.

Here is list of critical limits to help reinforce the important minimum times and temperatures needed to destroy the pathogens on food and control foodborne illness outbreaks. Other critical limits depending on your operation could be: humidity, water activity (moisture content), and acidity.

Remember our Chicken Soup? Let's re-cap...

- The **biological hazard** is *Salmonella* (highly contagious) and *Campylobacter*.
- The facilities SOP describes that a **preventive measure** is to cook the soup to kill any pathogens.
- A **critical control point** in the **flow of the food** is the cooking step for the chicken. Cooking is the kill step or the point where the destruction of harmful microorganisms occurs.
- The **critical limit** is to cook the soup to 165°F (73.9°C) for < 1 second to kill any *Salmonella* and *Campylobacter* on the chicken.

Minimum Internal Cooking Temperatures – Critical Limits

165°F (73.9°C) for < 1 second

- Reheat all leftover food to be hot held (for 15 seconds).
- Cook all poultry.
- Cook all stuffed products, including pasta.
- Foods cooked in a microwave, then let sit for 2 minutes.
- When combining already cooked and raw TCS products (casseroles).
- Cook all wild game animals.
- Cook all raw animal foods that have been partially cooked (no longer than 60 minutes and properly cooled).

155°F (68.3°C) for 17 Seconds or 158°F for < 1 second

Note: Check with your Manager

- Cook all ground: fish, beef, commercially raised game animals, ratites (emu, ostrich, and rhea), and pork.
- Cook all flavor-injected meats.
- Cook all eggs for hot holding and later service (buffet service).

145°F (62.8°C) for 15 Seconds

- Cook all fish and shellfish.
- Cook all intact meat such as chops/steaks of veal, beef, pork, commercially raised game animals, and lamb.
- Cook fresh eggs and egg products for immediate service.
- Cook roasts to 145°F for 4 minutes. (Roasting temperatures vary, see your manager for the proper procedure in your establishment.)

135°F (57.2°C)

- Fully cooked commercially processed products for hot holding.
- Cook vegetables and fruits for hot holding.

Did You Know...

Employees directly associated with or assigned to a particular part of the operation are often selected to monitor CCPs. Who else knows the procedures better than the person who does that task regularly?

Pop Quiz:
Critical Limits

Match the critical limit to the CCP by placing the letter that is most correct in the space provided.

1. If cooking is the CCP for a pork chop, what is the critical limit? _____

2. If cooling is the CCP for chicken soup, what is the critical limit? _____

3. If hot holding is the CCP for a chili, what is the critical limit? _____

4. If cooking is the CCP for a hamburger, what is the critical limit? _____

5. If cold holding is the CCP for tuna salad, what is the critical limit? _____

6. If cooking is the CCP for chicken soup, what is the critical limit? _____

7. If reheating is the CCP for chicken soup, what is the critical limit? _____

8. If cooking in the microwave is the CCP for fish, what is the critical limit? _____

9. If hot holding is the CCP for chicken soup, what is the critical limit? _____

10. If cooking is the CCP for stuffed fish, what is the critical limit? _____

a. The critical limit is 165°F (73.9°C) for < 1 second.

b. The critical limit is 165°F (73.9°C) for 15 seconds within 2 hours.

c. The critical limit is 155°F (68.3°C) for 17 seconds.

d. The critical limit is 145°F (62.8°C) for 15 seconds.

e. The critical limit is 135°F to 70°F (57.2°C to 21.1°C) within 2 hours; you then have an additional 4 hours to go from 70°F to 41°F (21.1°C to 5°C) or lower for a maximum total cool time of 6 hours.

f. The critical limit is below 41°F (5°C).

g. The critical limit is above 135°F (57.2°C).

HACCP Principle 4: Establish Monitoring Procedures

Monitoring procedures ensure that we are correctly meeting critical limits for the CCPs. This is the foundation for HACCP Principle 4. If we do not regularly check the CCPs, our HACCP plan may not be followed and the risk of foodborne illness increases. Monitoring enables the manager to determine if the team is doing its part to keep food safe. These procedures help to identify if there are equipment problems, product concerns, or refrigeration issues. Monitoring can be done through **measurement**, such as taking an internal product temperature of a food item. It can also be done by **making observations**. For example, documenting that date marking on deli meats was done properly and according to the SOP to control *Listeria*. This is by far the area in which you can shine the most as a HACCP team member— you make the difference in terms of whether or not your operation is serving safe food.

How to Monitor?

Your manager should have established **monitoring procedures** for a successful monitoring program. You should find these addressed in your SOPs. It is important to know your role and the roles of other team members.

- Is there a written SOP?
- Who will monitor the CCP(s)?
- What equipment and materials are needed?
- When should monitoring take place?
- How often should monitoring take place?
- How will the CCP(s) be monitored?

There are two kinds of monitoring:

- Continuous
- Non-continuous (Intermittent)

Continuous monitoring is a **constant** monitoring of a CCP. This is done with built-in measuring equipment that records time and temperatures. Computerized equipment systems are an example of continuous monitoring.

Non-continuous (Intermittent) monitoring is primarily what the majority of food service or retail operations use. This monitoring occurs at scheduled intervals. An example of non-continuous monitoring is using a properly calibrated thermometer to measure the temperature of chicken soup every 2 hours.

Understand Monitoring

Simply taking a food temperature reading without understanding the "Why" and "How" of the measurement is not a good practice and not an effective monitoring program. Taking food temperatures without knowing the critical limit is not part of an effective HACCP plan.

To have effective monitoring employees must:

- Request to be trained on monitoring procedures;
- Know how to use monitoring tools such as thermometers, test strips, and pH meters;
- Know the proper temperatures;

- Know other critical limits;
- Record monitoring results in logs; and
- Perform monitoring tasks for example every 2 hours or every 4 hours.

Use Monitoring Forms

In the HACCP system, proper documentation must be kept throughout the operational food flow. Documentation may not be a regulatory requirement in your state, but it is an essential part of a HACCP plan. Effectively using monitoring forms at receiving, storage, preparation, cooking, holding, cooling, and reheating stages provide a product history. This verifies that a product meets standards or indicates when adjustments to the system are needed. It also ensures that you have done all you can do to keep the food safe if a foodborne illness outbreak occurs. These records become the documentation for your regulatory agency; the media; and local, county, state, and federal food inspectors and is "proof" that you are doing things right and/or have made adjustments as needed to keep your CCP in check.

Equipment temperatures during meal preparation and service should be monitored at least every 4 hours; this includes all refrigeration, cooking, and holding equipment. If necessary, adjust the equipment thermostats so the food products meet the required temperature standards.

Other types of documentation include standard operating procedures, sanitation practices, employee practices, and employee training. This may be as simple as an informal notation of observations concerning what is working well and what is not working well. This documentation helps identify practices and procedures that may have to be modified or a need for additional employee training.

Did You Know...

Records are proof you are doing things correctly. Make sure you take and record measurements correctly. You never know when these records may be reviewed or needed for verification of the HACCP plan. Always record the good and the bad. Recording satisfactory measurements shows that a HACCP plan is being followed.

Receiving Deliveries—Monitoring (Sample SOP)

1. Inspect the delivery truck when it arrives to ensure that it is clean, free of putrid odors, and organized to prevent cross contamination. Be sure refrigerated foods are delivered in a refrigerated truck.

2. Check the interior temperature of refrigerated trucks.

3. Confirm vendor name, day and time of delivery, as well as driver's identification before accepting delivery. If the driver's name is different than what is indicated on the delivery schedule, contact the vendor immediately.

4. Check frozen foods to ensure that they are all frozen solid and show no signs of thawing and refreezing, such as the presence of large ice crystals or liquids on the bottom of cartons.

5. Check the temperature of refrigerated foods.
   a. For fresh meat, fish, dairy, and poultry products, insert a clean and sanitized thermometer into the center of the product to ensure a temperature of 41°F (5°C) or below.
   b. For packaged products, insert a food thermometer between two packages, being careful not to puncture the wrapper. If the temperature exceeds 41°F (5°C), it may be necessary to take the internal temperature before accepting the product.
   c. For eggs, the interior temperature of the truck should be 45°F (7.2°C) or below.

6. Check dates of milk, eggs, and other perishable goods to ensure safety and quality.

7. Check the integrity of food packaging.

8. Check the cleanliness of crates and other shipping containers before accepting products. Reject foods that are shipped in dirty crates.

Examples of Monitoring Forms

Thermometer Calibration Log:

DATE	THERMOMETER BEING CALIBRATED	TEMPERATURE	CORRECTIVE ACTION	EMPLOYEE INITIALS	MANAGER INTIALS AND DATE
06/11/17	Red001	32°F		AP	TP – 06/11/17
06/11/17	Blue001	32°F		TG	MV – 06/11/17
06/12/17	Red001	35°F	Ice water bath adjustment to 32°F	DD	TP – 06/12/17

Cooling Log:

Date	Employee Initials	Food	Time After 1 Hour	°F After 1 Hour	Time After 2 Hours	°F *Must* 70°F/ 21.1°C	Time After 3 Hours	°F After 3 Hours	Time After 4 Hours	°F After 4 Hours	Time After 5 Hours	°F After 5 Hours	Time After 6 Hours	°F

Cooking Log:

Date	Time	Food Product	Internal Temperature °F (°C)	Corrective Action Taken	Employee Initials	Manager Initials
	5 p.m.	Meatballs	158°F (70°C)			

FOOD FOR THOUGHT

Cooking Log

What is wrong with the Cooking Log? _____

_____

_____

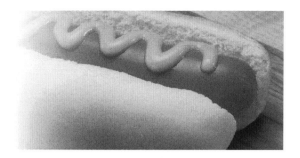

Star Knowledge Exercise:

Monitoring

What types of monitoring logs and food safety equipment would you need to have in place for the following foods? Place the appropriate letter(s) of the monitoring log(s) and equipment for each food item. Are there any additional logs or food safety equipment that you would use?

1. Chicken salad prepared on-site to be served that day.

Monitoring Logs:_____

Equipment: _____

2. Fish to be cooked on-site and served that day.

Monitoring Logs:_____

Equipment: _____

3. Chili prepared on-site to be served the next day.

Monitoring Logs:_____

Equipment: _____

Monitoring Logs

a. Receiving Log or Invoice (indicating temperature of frozen and/or refrigerated food as received)

b. Freezer Temperature Log

c. Refrigerator Temperature Log

d. Dry Storage Temperature Log

e. Preparation Temperature Log

f. Cooling Log

g. Reheating Log

h. Serving Line Temperature Log

i. Cooking Temperature Log

j. Cleaning Log

Equipment

k. Calibrated Thermometers

l. Heat Source: Oven, Stove, Grill, Microwave, Roller Grill, Broiler, Wok

m. Cold Holding Equipment

n. Cold Serving Equipment

o. Hot Holding Equipment

p. Hot Serving Equipment

q. Equipment to quickly cool food—ice bath, ice paddle, pans to reduce product portions for quicker cooling; or a Blast Chiller

Did You Know...

It is just as important to document your actions when things do not go according to plan. As well as, what corrective actions did you take to resolve a potential problem?

HACCP Principle 5: Identify Corrective Actions

 Now that the minimum and maximum limits have been identified and met through monitoring, we can identify the corrective actions necessary to fix the deficiencies. The **corrective actions** are predetermined steps that you automatically take if the critical limits are not being met. This principle describes what steps you take when something goes wrong. These predetermined steps will be laid out in the SOPs. This is HACCP Principle 5.

The following are examples of corrective actions:

- Reject a product that does not meet purchasing or receiving specifications.
- Reject a product that does not come from a reputable source.
- Test and fix thermometers when necessary on equipment such as refrigerators, freezers, ovens, hot holding carts, etc.
- Discard unsafe food products.
- Discard food if cross contamination occurs, especially if there is no cooking step.
- Continue cooking food until it reaches correct temperature.
- Reheat food to 165°F (73.9°C) for 15 seconds within 2 hours.
- Change methods of food handling to insure compliance.
- Train staff to calibrate thermometers and take temperatures properly.

Document: Write Everything Down!

Do not forget to record what you have done to correct any problems you have observed during monitoring. This practice is important and helpful. If a customer is stricken with a foodborne illness, you will need these documents as evidence of implementation of your HACCP system.

Sample Receiving Deliveries—Corrective Action (SOP)

1. Reject the following:
   a. Frozen foods with signs of previous thawing
   b. Cans that have signs of deterioration—swollen sides or ends, flawed seals or seams, dents, or rust
   c. Punctured packages
   d. Expired foods
   e. Foods that are out of safe temperature zone or deemed unacceptable by the established rejection policy

Use Corrective Action Forms

Sample Corrective Action Logs

Receiving Log: Date: 6/11/17

Time	Temp	Food Product Description	Product Code	Corrective Action Taken	Employee Initials	Manager Initials
8 AM	60°F	Eggs	007	Refuse Shipment	BE	TP

Cooling—Corrective Action Log:

Date	Food Product	Time	Temperature MUST: 70°F (21.1°C)–2 Hours MUST: 41°F (5°C)–6 Hours	Corrective Action Taken MUST: Reheat MUST: Discard	Employee Initials	Manager Initials

Refrigeration Log:

Date	Time	Type of Unit	Location	°F/°C	Corrective Action Taken	Employee Initials	Manager Initials

Did You Know...

No operation is perfect! Mistakes will happen. Knowing how to document and handle mistakes is critical to the success of your food service or retail establishment!

FOOD FOR THOUGHT

Corrective Action

The cook is preparing chicken soup that was made the previous day. She started to heat the soup at 8 a.m. in the jacketed steam kettle. She forgets to check the soup until 9:30 a.m., when she finds that the soup has reached 150°F (65.6°C). What does she need to do to be sure that the soup reaches the correct temperature for reheated foods? What could have caused the problem?

_____

_____

_____

_____

_____

_____

Star Point 4 Conclusion

In Star Point 4, we discussed why this step is the most important Star Point for you. This is where you make the greatest difference! You do that by "working the plan"—by monitoring, identifying, and facilitating corrective actions that in turn make food safe.

Star Point 4 Check for Understanding

(Circle one.)

1. The critical limit for chicken soup is _____ .
   a. cooking
   b. cooking to 165°F (73.9°C) for < 1 second
   c. washing your hands before you start cooking
   d. making sure to get your chicken from an approved source

2. Critical limits are _____ .
   a. based on science, measurable, and specific
   b. how fast you need to accomplish your daily tasks
   c. the act of observing or taking measurements to see if you CCPs are met
   d. none of the above

3. Times and temperatures of foods should be checked _____ .
   a. daily
   b. weekly
   c. every 12 hours
   d. every 2 – 4 hours

4. Corrective actions are _____ .
   a. telling your team member about the problem and hoping they will fix it
   b. never throwing away food because food is too expensive
   c. actions taken when CCPs are not met
   d. can wait for the next shift to correct

5. When monitoring CCPs, employees should _____ .
   a. decide which CCPs to monitor that day
   b. purchase their own equipment and tools needed to monitor the CCP
   c. change which CCPs are monitored frequently
   d. always follow monitoring SOPs

HACCP Star Point 5:
HACCP Principles 6 & 7 – Confirm by Verification, Record Keeping, and Documentation

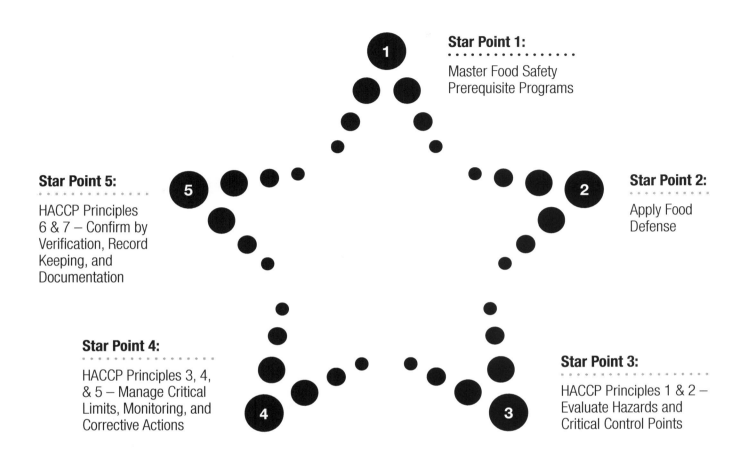

Star Point 1:
Master Food Safety Prerequisite Programs

Star Point 2:
Apply Food Defense

Star Point 3:
HACCP Principles 1 & 2 – Evaluate Hazards and Critical Control Points

Star Point 4:
HACCP Principles 3, 4, & 5 – Manage Critical Limits, Monitoring, and Corrective Actions

Star Point 5:
HACCP Principles 6 & 7 – Confirm by Verification, Record Keeping, and Documentation

Star Point 5 Myth or Fact (Check one.)

1. Verification confirms, record keeping proves.
___**Myth** ___**Fact**

2. Record keeping will verify your HACCP plan is working.
___**Myth** ___**Fact**

3. Verification of a HACCP plan is done by all employees.
___**Myth** ___**Fact**

4. You can verify a HACCP plan by observing employees preforming tasks.
___**Myth** ___**Fact**

5. You should keep all records for a one month period.
___**Myth** ___**Fact**

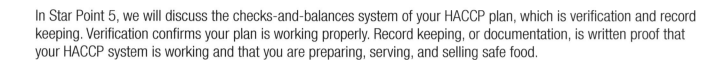

Star Point 5 Goals

You will learn to:

- Confirm/verify that the system works (HACCP Principle 6); and
- Maintain records and documentation (HACCP Principle 7).

In Star Point 5, we will discuss the checks-and-balances system of your HACCP plan, which is verification and record keeping. Verification confirms your plan is working properly. Record keeping, or documentation, is written proof that your HACCP system is working and that you are preparing, serving, and selling safe food.

HACCP Principle 6: Verify That the System Works

Verification is confirmation that the steps of the plan are working. This is the basis of HACCP Principle 6. It ensures that your operation is maintaining an effective food safety program, and it provides an opportunity to update the plan as needed. Verification will be completed by the supervisor, director, or even an outside firm.

Verification includes specific actions:

- Who will perform them?
- What needs to be performed?
- Where will this be performed?
- When will they be performed?
- Why? Verification confirms that the HACCP plan is working!
- How will they be performed?
- How will they be documented?

Verification is necessary when:

- New food preparation practices are introduced.
  - Adding banquet services
  - Adding catering services
  - Adding rotisserie chicken
  - Adding a frying process to the food service or retail operation.
- New equipment is added to the kitchen;
- New food items have been added to the menu;
- A foodborne illness is believed to be associated with a food;
- A foodborne illness has been reported;
- Personnel changes; and
- Changes are made to the Food Code/Regulations. For instance, every two years the Food Code is updated. This is a good time to update HACCP plans.

Here are some ways to verify a HACCP plan:

- Observe employees performing tasks, especially monitoring CCPs;
- Check critical control point records;
- Review monitoring records;
- Check equipment temperatures;
- Review hazard analysis and CCPs;
- Understand why foods have not reached their critical limits; and
- Determine causes for equipment failure and procedure failure.

As a food service or retail employee, realize that a new menu or a concept change will require verification and changes to your HACCP plan. Verification is important because it reviews every Star Point and confirms that your HACCP plan is working.

HACCP Principle 7: Record Keeping and Documentation

To complete the final HACCP principle, you must document any corrective actions taken and record measurements used while monitoring the flow of food. This documentation begins at delivery to the facility, and continues through the service to the customer and shows the food product being monitored. The final HACCP principle involves all the paperwork, documents, logs, etc., that you have maintained as you have monitored the flow of food.

Records have several benefits, they:

- Provide a source of information about day in and day out operations;
- Provide long term trends when analyzed;
- Show CCPs are being met;
- Confirm when and what corrective actions have been taken; and
- Provide valuable information or proof of compliance if a foodborne illness occurs.

It is critical when documenting to get enough information to ensure your HACCP plan is effective. All records must be accurate and legible. **Never** scribble or use correction tape or liquid because it may look like a cover up. For errors, always draw a line through the mistake and initial. Never falsify records or resources (dry labbing).

Did You Know...

Dry labbing is filling out forms or logs without taking any actual measurements. These are falsified documents and you could lose your job and in some cases, face criminal prosecution.

In order to be effective, your record keeping plans should include the following:

- HACCP Plan
- Standardized Recipes
- SOPs
- Monitoring Procedures
- Shellstock Tags
- Grinding Log (Lot #'s)
- Equipment Maintenance Log
- List of Approved Chemicals
- Forms
- Invoices
- Schedules
- Company Organization Chart
- Serving Line Temperature Log
- Cold Holding Equipment Temperature Log
- Hot Holding Equipment Temperature Log
- Cold Serving Equipment Temperature Log
- Hot Serving Equipment Temperature Log
- Dry Storage Temperature Log
- Calibrated Thermometers Log
- Master Cleaning Checklist
- Receiving Temperature Log
- Freezer Temperature Log
- Discard Log (waste chart/shrink log)
- Pest Control Documentation
- Employee Health Records
- Cooking Temperature Log
- Checklists (Food Safety, Work Station Procedures, Operational Steps)
- Corrective actions taken to correct the problem
- Records of employee training
- Flow Charts
- Specifications of the food products

Sample Record Keeping Logs

The following are samples of forms used for record keeping:

Thermometer Calibration Log:

Date	Employee	A.M. Time	Mid Time	P.M. Time	Date	Employee	A.M. Time	Mid Time	P.M. Time

Reheating Log:

Date	Time	Food Product	Internal Temperature	Corrective Action Taken	Employee Initials	Manager Initials

Discard Log:

Date	Time	Food Product Description	• Hold • Discard • Return • Credit	Explain Action Taken Reason	Employee Initials	Manager Initials

Record keeping provides us with a history showing that we are following prerequisite programs and the 7 HACCP Principles. By documenting these steps, we are proving that we are consistently preparing, serving, and selling safe food.

Sample SOP For Receiving

Receiving Deliveries (Sample SOP)

Purpose: To ensure that all food is received fresh and safe when it enters the food service or retail operation, and to transfer food to proper storage as quickly as possible.

Scope: This procedure applies to food service or retail employees who are responsible for receiving food products into the establishment.

Key Words: Cross contamination, temperatures, receiving, holding, frozen goods, delivery

Instructions:

1. Train food service or retail employees who accept deliveries on proper receiving procedures.

2. Schedule deliveries to arrive at designated times during operational hours.

3. Post the delivery schedule, including the names of vendors, days and times of deliveries, and drivers' names.

4. Establish a rejection policy to ensure accurate, timely, consistent, and effective refusal and return of rejected goods.

5. Organize freezer and refrigeration space, loading docks, and storage rooms before deliveries.

6. Before deliveries, gather product specification lists and purchase orders, temperature logs, calibrated thermometers, pens, flashlights, and clean loading carts.

7. Keep receiving area clean and well lighted.

8. Do not touch ready-to-eat foods with bare hands.

9. Determine whether foods will be marked with the date of arrival or the "use-by" date and mark accordingly upon receipt.

10. Compare delivery invoice against products ordered and products delivered.

11. Transfer foods to their appropriate locations as quickly as possible.

Monitoring:

1. Inspect the delivery truck when it arrives to ensure that it is clean, free of putrid odors, and organized to prevent cross contamination. Be sure refrigerated foods are delivered on a refrigerated truck.

2. Check the interior temperature of refrigerated trucks.

3. Confirm vendor name, day and time of delivery, as well as driver's identification before accepting delivery. If the driver's name is different than what is indicated on the delivery schedule, contact the vendor immediately.

4. Check frozen foods to ensure that they are all frozen solid and show no signs of thawing and refreezing, such as the presence of large ice crystals or liquids on the bottom of cartons.

5. Check the temperature of refrigerated foods.

   a. For fresh meat, fish, dairy, and poultry products, insert a clean and sanitized thermometer into the center of the product to ensure a temperature of 41ºF (5°C) or below.

   b. For packaged products, insert a food thermometer between two packages, being careful not to puncture the wrapper. If the temperature exceeds 41ºF (5°C), it may be necessary to take the internal temperature before accepting the product.

   c. For eggs, the interior temperature of the truck should be 45ºF (7.2°C) or below.

6. Check sell by dates of milk, eggs, and other perishable goods to ensure safety and quality.

7. Check the integrity of food packaging. Make sure all packaging is unopened and shows no signs of tampering.

8. Check the cleanliness of crates and other shipping containers before accepting products. Reject foods that are shipped in dirty crates.

Corrective Action:

Reject the following:

a. Frozen foods with signs of previous thawing

b. Cans that have signs of deterioration—swollen sides or ends, flawed seals or seams, dents, or rust

c. Punctured packages

d. Expired foods

e. Foods that are out of the safe temperature zone or deemed unacceptable by the established rejection policy

Verification and Record Keeping:

When the food service or retail operation receives food, they must record temperatures and any corrective actions taken on the delivery invoice or on the receiving log. The food service or retail manager will verify that food service or retail employees are receiving products using the proper procedure by visually monitoring receiving practices during the shift and reviewing the receiving log at the close of each day. Receiving logs are kept on file for a minimum of one year.

Date Implemented: _____ By: _____

Date Reviewed: _____ By: _____

Date Revised: _____ By: _____

Verification

Check the box when verification should be done to evaluate the HACCP plan.

☐ 1. New menu items or recipes

☐ 2. New uniforms

☐ 3. New equipment

☐ 4. New food preparation procedure

☐ 5. New shelving added to reorganize storage

Star Point 5 Conclusion

In Star Point 5, we discussed the checks and balances system of your HACCP plan's verification and record keeping. Verification confirms your plan is working properly. Record keeping is proof that your HACCP plan is working properly.

Star Point 5 Check for Understanding
(Circle one.)

1. HACCP principle 7 is _____ .
   a. hazard analysis
   b. verification
   c. record keeping
   d. monitoring

2. Verification includes _____ .
   a. who will perform the verification task
   b. when verification will be preformed
   c. how verification will be documented
   d. all of the above

3. Record keeping involves _____ .
   a. having the phone number so you can call off work
   b. all paperwork, documents, and logs, that have been maintained as the food flow is monitored
   c. filling in random numbers on the log sheets when you are running behind schedule
   d. getting rid of document at the end of the week

4. When you keep records you should _____ .
   a. never scribble on forms or log sheets
   b. never dry lab
   c. always neatly cross out mistakes
   d. all of the above

5. HACCP principle 6 is _____ .
   a. hazard analysis
   b. verification
   c. record keeping
   d. monitoring

Conclusion

Are You a HACCP "All-Star"?

The goal of this manual was to help you, the participant, better understand the five points in the HACCP Star and to demonstrate how each point has helped you use an effective HACCP plan. Now that you have a better understanding of a HACCP plan, it is up to you to be a valued HACCP team member by applying the prerequisite programs and the HACCP principles learned in this book to your everyday work life.

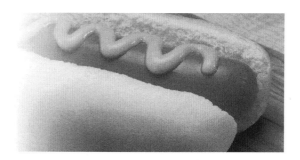

Star Knowledge Exercise:

7 HACCP Principle Match Game

Match the HACCP number with the HACCP principle by placing the correct letter in the space provided.

HACCP Principle 1: _____

HACCP Principle 2: _____

HACCP Principle 3: _____

HACCP Principle 4: _____

HACCP Principle 5: _____

HACCP Principle 6: _____

HACCP Principle 7: _____

a. Establish Record Keeping and Documentation Procedures

b. Identify Corrective Actions

c. Conduct a Hazard Analysis

d. Establish Critical Limits

e. Determine Critical Control Points

f. Establish Verification Procedures

g. Establish Monitoring Procedures

7 HACCP Principles Match Game Results

How many points did you earn? _____

If you scored 7 points—Congratulations! You are a HACCP Principles All-Star!

If you scored 5–6 points—Good job! You have a basic understanding of HACCP principles.

If you scored 3–4 points—The time to review is now! What a great opportunity to fine-tune your HACCP principles skills.

If you scored 0–2 points—You should discuss with your trainer ways to better understand the HACCP principles so, that you may apply them at your establishment to serve and sell safe food.

It is time to take your HACCP examination to test your understanding of this program. Upon successful completion of the examination, you will receive your HACCP All-Star Certificate. The HACCP certification is valid for four years and is recognized as basic HACCP comprehension for employees. Please complete the evaluation on your trainer and prepare to take your HACCP examination.

Answer Key

HACCP Pre-Test (Pages 6-7)

1.	b.	**6.**	b.	**11.**	c.
2.	b.	**7.**	b.	**12.**	a.
3.	c.	**8.**	a.	**13.**	c.
4.	c.	**9.**	a.	**14.**	b.
5.	c.	**10.**	a.	**15.**	a.

Star Point 1 Myth or Fact Answers (Page 9)

1. Myth
2. Fact
3. Fact
4. Myth
5. Fact

Star Point 1 Check for Understanding Answers (Page 46)

1. d. Hazard Analysis and Critical Control Point
2. a. Acceptable practices and procedures for your operation
3. d. Hepatitis B
4. a. 41°F – 135°F (5°C – 57.2°C)
5. c. Define acceptable practices and procedures for the entire food service or retail establishment and its employees

Star Point 2 Myth or Fact Answers (Page 47)

1. Myth
2. Fact
3. Fact
4. Fact
5. Myth

Star Point 2 Check for Understanding Answers (Page 54)

1. d. All of the above
2. b. Preventing intentional contamination to food
3. c. Having a 2 year supply of food
4. d. Both b and c
5. b. Employee health awareness

Star Point 3 Myth or Fact Answers (Page 55)

1. Fact
2. Fact
3. Fact
4. Myth
5. Fact

Star Point 3 Check for Understanding Answers (Page 69)

1. c. Control Point (CP)
2. b. Simple/No-Cook, Same-Day, and Complex
3. b. Food safety
4. b. One of the last steps where you can prevent, eliminate, or reduce a food safety hazard
5. b. Chocolate Chip Cookie

Star Point 4 Myth or Fact Answers (Page 71)

1. Fact
2. Myth
3. Fact
4. Myth
5. Fact

Star Point 4 Check for Understanding Answers (Page 82)

1. b. Cooking to 165°F (73.8°C) for 15 seconds
2. a. Based on science, measurable, and specific
3. d. Every 2 – 4 hours
4. c. Actions taken when CCPs are not met
5. d. Always follow monitoring SOPs

Star Point 5 Myth or Fact Answers (Page 83)

1. Fact
2. Myth
3. Myth
4. Fact
5. Myth

Answer Key

Star Point 5 Check for Understanding Answers (Page 91)

1. c. Record Keeping
2. d. All of the above
3. b. All paperwork, documents, and logs, that have been maintained as the food flow is monitored
4. d. All of the above
5. b. Verification

Star Knowledge Exercise:
7 HACCP Principle Match Game (Page 94)

HACCP Principle 1. c.

HACCP Principle 2. e.

HACCP Principle 3. d.

HACCP Principle 4. g.

HACCP Principle 5. b.

HACCP Principle 6. f.

HACCP Principle 7. a.